PRAISE FOR BRIGADIER GENERAL JOHN "DRAGON" TEICHERT AND BOOM!

"*BOOM!* is an excellent book on leadership and it resonates at all levels. It is more than just a collection of personal experiences—Dragon brings a career's worth of thoughtful and honest analysis of lessons with a wealth of practical applications. This is a valuable read for any leader."

—Lieutenant General Kevin "Gumby" Schneider
United States Air Force

"Dragon Teichert, General Chuck Yeager's friend, wonderfully embodies the spirit of America's Hero in his effective and innovative leadership style. In this captivating book, Dragon provides a creative venue that delivers how-to details to help leaders everywhere inspire innovation and break barriers."

—Mrs. Chuck "Victoria" Yeager
author, pilot, businesswoman

"It's a rare opportunity for Americans to learn and gain invaluable insight and lessons from such a great American. Dragon's journey as a leader in the military, the community and as a family man and Christian has been a massive benefit to our Nation. I'm proud to call him a friend and hope more Americans follow his example!"

—Congressman Mike "Ponch" Garcia
California's 27th Congressional District

"Great read! At Lockheed Martin, I had a front row seat to the remarkable innovation and cultural change that Dragon was able to achieve during his time at Edwards Air Force Base. This book tells not just the story of that journey, but how you as a leader can get the same exceptional results. His ideas are applicable to all; I intend to steal a few!"

—**Jeff Babione**
Head Skunk (2018-22), Lockheed Martin Skunk Works

"Having soared the skies and served shoulder-to-shoulder with John 'Dragon' Teichert, I can attest to his remarkable knack for shattering the barriers of bureaucracy. *BOOM!* isn't just a read—it's a flight plan for those ready to take off, filled with tales of jet fuel, sonic booms, unwavering leadership, and innovation at Mach speed. If you feel like your organization is stuck on the runway, this book is your afterburner!"

—**Brigadier General Derek "Maestro" O'Malley**
United States Air Force

"Dragon's *BOOM!* is authentically him in all the best ways: energetic genius, tethered by high-strength historical examples & anecdotal proofs-of-concept…all laser-focused on harnessing the strength and capability of others through empowering leadership. He writes as he leads: generously sharing his vision and toolkit for success, hoping only to spur (in his own words) a 'continuing advantage' of progress using the potential he unfailingly sees in those around him. His style is engaging & easy to follow, with each chapter anchored with Action Items…think former Navy SEAL David Goggins but for innovation & leadership vs. grit & perseverance. If you want to cut through red tape, inspire solutions and progress, and bring the whole team with you, *BOOM!* is the best handbook you'll find anywhere, written by a truly inspiring Air Force leader!"

—**Colonel Lisa "Demetri" Mabbutt**
United States Air Force

"John Teichert uses the same skills in *BOOM!* that I witnessed him deliver a hundred times in person; part erudite, part everyman, with a keen understanding of how to communicate with everyone in his sphere.

He does the same here, seamlessly blending the past, present and even the future, with wit, candor and an emphasis on the value of teamwork, to weave an understanding of a leadership style that is uniquely Dragon while combining the best attributes of a lifetime studying successful leadership at its core.

The book is entertaining and engaging, and answers, in ways that easily reach any reader, why each leadership style is effective in a range of differing scenarios, and why learning, in all its forms, continues long after we leave the classroom."

—M. H. Jim Estepp
former Chair, Prince George's County Council

"A must-read for leaders and the led, who, with the right leader or opportunity, can unlock unknown potential! Brig Gen (ret) Teichert, a proven leader, takes you on a journey of his leadership experiences and how his listen, consider, and act cycle inspired an innovation movement! Having worked under his leadership, I can attest to the profound impact the action items listed throughout this book had on his ability to inspire multiple U. S. Government agencies and foreign leaders, whose relationship could be tense, to work together to achieve common objectives for the greater good. How do you inspire your idea champions? Read to find out—maybe starting with a little 'dad joke' will work. It worked for those of us who had the honor of working for Dragon!"

—Colonel Phylishia South
U.S. Army

"*BOOM!* is an excellent read revealing steps of innovation to accelerate America's Air Force; proven leadership principles and examples every leader needs to hear and place into frequent action; and a foundation of unleashing, empowering and resourcing ordinary people who accomplished extraordinary results!"

—Tony Rubino

"A practical guide to shifting culture set against the rich history of Edwards Air Force Base and the United States Air Force, *BOOM! Leadership that Breaks Barriers, Challenges Convention, and Ignites Innovation* belongs on the shelf of every innovative leader."

—Heidi Williams
Inaugural Leader of the Hustle Squad (the innovation team at Edwards AFB)

"Dragon's gripping exploration of leadership is both profound and rooted in real-world experiences. Through a masterful blend of inspiration and practical wisdom, he offers invaluable insights into the decades-long journey of leadership. An essential read for aspiring and sitting leaders everywhere."

—Ian Eishen
Command Chief, Edwards Air Force Base (2019–2021)

"Riveting! A book about leadership written by a true servant leader that takes you on a journey weaving in and out of brilliantly-told stories of innovation! The Hustle Squad's lessons in applied leadership will leave leaders in any industry the blueprint to drive innovation. I served with Dragon and witnessed his leadership style in real time. This is a must read!"

—Dr. Nathaniel M. Perry
Dean, College of Military Studies and Leadership, Columbia Southern University

"Leading culture change is hard - really HARD! Brig Gen (ret) E. John 'Dragon' Teichert's *BOOM!* provides an exciting, impactful and easy-to-implement action plan to accelerate innovation and unleash your team by listening, considering and acting! All leaders will benefit from the keen insights and experiences shared in *BOOM!*"

—General (ret) Stephen "Seve" Wilson
USAF Vice Chief of Staff (2016–2020)

"I highly recommend *BOOM!* Dragon's revolutionary approach and cutting-edge techniques unleashed his workforce and ignited creativity, and I know it will inspire countless others to break down barriers and accomplish the unthinkable."

—**Wendy E. Newby**
Senior National Security Executive, Central Intelligence Agency (ret)

"*BOOM!* is a user's guide to leadership! Dragon Teichert contextualizes leadership through historical narratives and sage advice while highlighting action items that put the power of his brand of transformational leadership into the hands of anyone. Whether you are a strategist or a practitioner, this is an essential read!"

—**Jason Korman**
CEO, Gapingvoid Culture Design Group

"How does a senior leader, especially one of intimidating position and rank, create and sustain a culture of innovation? That's the question Brigadier General (ret.) John "Dragon" Teichert answers in *BOOM!* The surge of innovations that emerged under Dragon's leadership were militarily significant. But what makes *BOOM!* valuable for leaders of any organization is Teichert's account of how he and his team went all in to unleash a spirit of innovation, and then built a system to capture and take advantage of the many ideas that emerged. A believer in servant leadership and the listen, consider, act cycle, Teichert walked the talk by engaging personally and repeatedly with many different communities, even dressing up as judge with a powdered wig to publicly assess new ideas. Asked late in his tenure what was the best idea that the innovation sprint had produced, Teichert's answer was people-centered: it was the decision to listen to all new ideas."

—**Ambassador (ret) Brian D. McFeeters**
U.S. Ambassador to Malaysia (2021-2023)

"Leading can be difficult. John Teichert makes it look easy, but it's not. I arrived at the Air Force Test Center soon after John took command of the 412th Test Wing, and watched with admiration as he harnessed the pioneering spirit of his amazing team…a team needing only to find their power to break barriers.

John is a brilliant servant-leader who has risked his life in combat, defied the odds as a test pilot, and influenced the global order as commander of an international coalition in harm's way. His is a spirit of sacrifice… sacrifice for the welfare of his Nation and humanity. John's beacon has thus far shone on America's Airmen who build the Airpower that keeps our Nation safe. But his wisdom can be a force multiplier for any enterprise, any undertaking in life. Thankfully, John has shared his wisdom in this book.

What does innovation look like? It looks like an organization producing well above the sum of its parts. An enterprise exuding world-class risk management in an era of unprecedented volatility. A group overflowing with individuals fulfilled by their unique contributions to a high-performing team, undistracted by misguided pursuits common in the world today.

Those who know John are eagerly awaiting the next target for his energy and talent. His roadmap for transformation is a game-changer. John's teams are empowered, inspired, resourced, and operate with a sense of urgency to deliver off-the-chart results. If you want the same for your team, listen to Dragon!"

—**Major General (ret) Christopher P. Azzano**
Air Force Test Center Commander (2018–2021)

BOOM!

Leadership that Breaks Barriers, Challenges Convention, and Ignites Innovation

---

JOHN "DRAGON" TEICHERT
US AIR FORCE BRIGADIER GENERAL (RET)

Copyright © 2023 John Teichert

All rights reserved.

No part of this publication may be reproduced, distributed, or transmitted in any form or by any means, including photocopying, recording, or other electronic or mechanical methods, without the prior written permission of the author, except in the case of brief quotations embodied in critical reviews and certain other noncommercial uses permitted by copyright law. For written permission visit www.johnteichert.com.

Editor: Lauren Mix of LMEditing—www.LMEditingservices.com

Publisher: Capital Leadership Books

ISBN: 979-8-218-31786-7

The views expressed in this publication are those of the author and do not necessarily reflect the official policy or position of the Department of Defense or the U.S. government.

The public release clearance of this publication by the Department of Defense does not imply Department of Defense endorsement or factual accuracy of the material.

The appearance of U.S. Department of Defense visual information does not imply or constitute DOD endorsement.

TABLE OF CONTENTS

Prologue
A Hypothetical Wartime Scenario, Saved by Innovation . . 1

Introduction
Innovation on Afterburner 5

Chapter One
Breaking Glass 11

Chapter Two
Street Signs and Quick Wins 21

Chapter Three
Unleashing the Team 29

Chapter Four
Sufficient Runway 39

Chapter Five
Your Calendar and Your Checkbook 45

Chapter Six
Charging the Hill 53

Chapter Seven
Dad Jokes 61

Chapter Eight
An Innovation Manifesto 71

Chapter Nine
#innovativeAF (AF Means Air Force) 81

Chapter Ten
Spikes on a Wire 97

Chapter Eleven
A Message in the Misfortunes 109

Chapter Twelve
Trial by Dragon 119

Chapter Thirteen
Non-Material Solutions 129

Chapter Fourteen
Shared Humanity and Mutual Benefit 137

Chapter Fifteen
Your Greatest Idea 151

Chapter Sixteen
Daring Wins! 159

Chapter Seventeen
Continuing Advantage 169

Endnotes 177

Acknowledgments 185

About the Author 187

PROLOGUE

A HYPOTHETICAL WARTIME SCENARIO, SAVED BY INNOVATION

In early July 2027, Western intelligence sources pick up unambiguous signals that the Chinese Communist Party (CCP) has directed preparation for an imminent military attack to seize Taiwan through an airborne and amphibious assault on August 1st, the centennial anniversary of the People's Liberation Army (PLA) itself. There are no indications suggesting that this is a drill as the Chinese political environment has made this the perfect outlet for such unbridled aggression.

Long term Communist Party Chairman, Xi Jinping is pleased with the military modernization milestones achieved by the PLA and believes that their advanced capabilities, geographic proximity to the rogue island, and sizable numerical advantage are enough to overwhelm any attempts to thwart their long-desired plans for reunification.

In response to the credible intelligence, United States Indo-Pacific Command implements their preparatory war planning efforts, hoping that a strong and resolute reaction will maintain the fragile posture of deterrence that prevents deadly conflict. Recognizing the extreme vulnerability of large American military bases in the western Pacific to an advanced Chinese missile barrage expected at the outset of the conflict, the United States Air Force (USAF) is directed to utilize a concept called Agile Combat Employment (ACE).

Created in the 2010s, ACE distributes air assets to smaller airfields throughout the region, turning a few big targets into a slew of smaller targets, complicating the targeting of any preemptive strike that could end the war before it even begins. This is quite an assignment, practiced extensively over the past few years, in anticipation of a potential large-scale conflict with China that everyone hoped would never come.

The key to the ACE concept is a cadre of USAF personnel trained to operate in small numbers at these distributed airfields to engage in a wide range of support activities that normally require a much larger manpower footprint at a traditional base. These airmen must provide for their own security while refueling combat aircraft, reloading weapons, providing air traffic control, and managing small-scale logistics at their location.

One of the trickiest components of the ACE concept is ensuring the ability to safely provide maintenance support to all aircraft in the Air Force, Navy, and allied inventory that may arrive at every possible disbursed location. While months of training are typically necessary to gain the skill set required to perform maintenance and weapons activities on a single type of modern-day flying machine, these ACE experts may only have hours to prepare to do so for a variety of aircraft under combat conditions, which could include incoming missile fire and working under the cover of darkness. Success in the conflict largely depends on the ACE experts sufficiently executing this challenging role.

Instead of utilizing paper checklists and hard copy diagrams to learn their aircraft maintenance tasks, the ACE experts use a more modern approach. Virtual reality (VR) software kits are used to simulate the exact maintenance tasks, which are coupled with augmented reality (AR) capabilities to overlay virtual, visual instructions onto real aircraft. Through the VR/AR goggles, a virtual expert talks these ACE professionals through each action and every step, offering explicit, detailed guidance to quickly refuel, repair, and reload a slew of aircraft types to get them back into the fight quickly—turning novices into aces!

A large part of this revolutionary support capability originated at Edwards Air Force Base in the Mojave Desert, nearly a decade before the current looming conflict with China, from the minds of several professionals during an innovation movement that contagiously swept the base.

Technical Sergeant Jeremy Neilson began experimenting with VR/AR technology in his free time while managing the regular training program of F-35 maintainers at the base. He believed that the future of American warfare depended on it, though the Air Force had yet to embrace his forward-thinking concept. Neilson's vision for the necessity of this capability was so compelling that it took him far outside his assigned responsibilities, and he couldn't resist tinkering, experimenting, and innovating, especially having been given the latitude and resources to do so.

Meanwhile, restless F-22 maintainer Staff Sergeant Michael Meyer had joined the Hustle Squad, a newly formed innovation team at Edwards Air Force Base. He began pouring his time, energy, expertise and attention into the non-traditional, innovative activity that was transforming a core part of the base wide culture.

Meyer quickly and eagerly linked up with Neilson's efforts, and the duo became a force of intellect, enthusiasm, and vision. The VR/AR ideas resonated with Meyer so much that he carried the concepts with him when a normal military move transferred him to a base in northern Texas to train new F-22 maintainers, landing him in the heart of the training enterprise of the entire United States Air Force. He used this opportunity to broadcast his experiences and the activity he witnessed in its infancy at Edwards to catch the attention of the right leaders and get the VR/AR concept adopted as part of the regular training establishment for all maintenance personnel throughout the force.

The 2027 distributed aircraft posture that flows from the ACE concept in the western Pacific has a real chance of sustainable success thanks to

Neilson, Meyer and their open-minded colleagues. It doesn't guarantee that the war will be won by Taiwan, the United States, and their allies and partners, but the CCP-controlled forces would be almost impossible to stop without this and other innovations.

Perhaps, because of the distributed force support capability that is the backbone of ACE, Xi Jinping will reconsider his attack plans before it is too late, allowing peace to prevail. If it does, a large extent of that success could be traced back to a powerful experiment in leadership, innovation, and organizational transformation at Edwards Air Force Base, a place that has come to be known as The Center of the Aerospace Testing Universe.

INTRODUCTION

INNOVATION ON AFTERBURNER

As a young boy, I was fascinated by four things: dinosaurs, rockets, airplanes, and volcanoes. I studied them obsessively. Before my first-grade year, I was thrilled to find out that my family was moving to a new home on "the ring of fire" in western Washington state and even more excited to learn that there was an active volcano, called Mount Saint Helens, just 100 miles to the south with a high likelihood of erupting.

At the time of our move, everyone in the area was focused on this daunting potential. The dome of volcanic material growing in the crater of the mountain was described daily by the local news. Experts were quick to provide their projections of the looming eruption date. Authorities had established a mandatory evacuation order around the base of the mountain, directing all residents and visitors to a safe distance until further notice. There were even songs by local bands chronicling the impending disaster.

As far as I can remember, there was only one person who refused to abide by the evacuation order. Not to be confused with President Harry S. Truman, old-timer Harry R. Truman, owner of Spirit Lake Lodge at the base of the mountain, famously, defiantly, and complacently stood his ground and said, "The mountain ain't going to hurt me." However, around 8:30 on the beautiful morning of May 18th, 1980, it did.

Boom! Before the thunderous explosion that accompanied the anticipated eruption had even reached my 7-year-old ears, Truman was covered by over 150 feet of volcanic debris. No one has seen him or Spirit Lake Lodge since. Later that same day, I had an unobstructed view of the massive mushroom cloud of ash being thrust into the upper atmosphere and carried by the prevailing winds around the planet. It was an awe-inspiring sight that I will never forget.

We live in a world that is constantly changing, and those who don't move with it will be left behind. It is happening at all levels—from local to state to national to global—in business, community planning, medicine, science, technology, government, communication, finance, education, and even national security strategy and policy. The defiant get buried by their competitors. Upstarts, not even worth a passing consideration, overtake the larger, complacent organizations that blindly follow the comfortable and alluring path of the status quo.

Alternatively, by boldly leading our organizations into the future erupting with change, we can avoid being buried. By unleashing the talent and creativity of our teams, we can bury the competition. By breaking barriers, challenging convention, and igniting innovation, we can harness the explosion of progress.

Leaders, light the afterburners of innovation to accelerate boldly and successfully into the future!

Afterburners are specialized components of certain jet engines, typically used on advanced military aircraft, like the kind flown by Maverick and crew in Top Gun. These features, which are bolted onto the back end of high-performance engines, dump raw fuel into the exhaust chamber, providing a massive increase in thrust.

Afterburners allow an aircraft to rapidly accelerate to its maximum performance, ultimately butting against the envelope of the aircraft limits determined by design engineers and validated by USAF test pilots to ensure that an aircraft safely and effectively performs to the fullest extent of its capabilities. Many of these test flights are performed in the Mojave Desert at Edwards Air Force Base—The Center of the Aerospace Testing Universe—an amazing place with an incredible mission.

This book is about my experience as the commander of The Center of Aerospace Testing Universe, where test pilots and engineers mold and shape America's aerospace arsenal. It is in this remote location that the United States Air Force, the United States Space Force, sister military services, NASA, and ally and partner nations test aircraft and spacecraft at the edge of the envelope, including fighters, bombers, tankers, transports, trainers, unmanned aerial systems, rockets, autonomous systems, artificial-intelligence enhanced aircraft, revolutionary weapons, and other emerging technologies.

Despite the cutting-edge nature of the mission at Edwards, it was not unlike any other bureaucratic organization when I first arrived. Even at a place boldly called The Center of the Aerospace Testing Universe, severe barriers to innovation stood in the way of progress, causing the storied location to fall far short of its true potential.

However, beginning in 2018, a different type of test took place at this hallowed ground of aerospace history that provided the ideal evaluation of a concept that transcended aircraft and rockets. It enabled the perfect proof of concept for organizational transformation that created a culture of innovation and broke the barriers of bureaucracy.

Its effect resounded through the Air Force like a booming shock wave radiating from an aircraft racing through the sky faster than the speed of sound. In a thundering turnaround, Edwards Air Force Base proved the potency and power of turbo-charged transformation and innovation at scale. It plugged in the afterburners and quickly explored the edge of the organizational performance envelope.

The results astonished all onlookers, dwarfing the innovation activity of the rest of the United States Air Force combined. Boom!

It sounds incredible, and, as a test pilot, I know the power of proving conclusions with data. Figure 1.0 illustrates an incredible story that I will tell in the pages to follow.

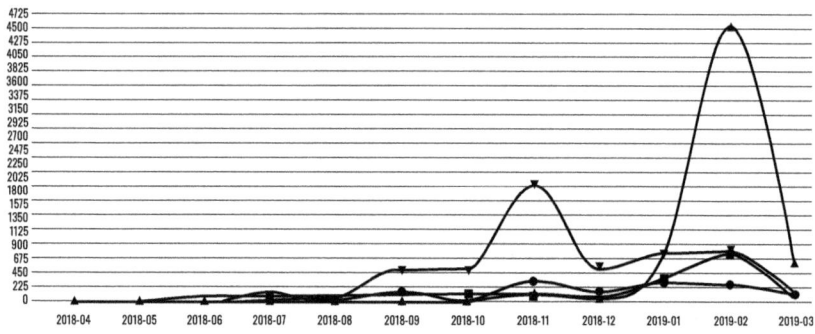

Figure 1.0

The mountain of innovation activity on the graph reflects the results of our initial 70-day experiment among our population of 11,000 personnel at The Center of the Aerospace Testing Universe. The tiny molehills that make up the majority of the rest of the graph are the innovation campaigns of our counterpart organizations around the Air Force. The only other sizable peak, though still much smaller than ours, is a campaign championed by the U.S. Air Force headquarters with the full weight of authority, priority and interest of a massive 670,000-person organization.

The combined innovation efforts of our counterpart organizations and the Air Force headquarters pale in comparison to our single organization's mountain of innovation activity. Our focused campaign employed a unique trial of proven leadership principles interwoven with some unorthodox methods available to all who are brave and wise enough to employ them. And that was just the beginning!

This book is a description of our journey and those methods. It is not a self-serving exposé of the leadership of a single commander, so please don't consider this as an unobtainable journey for you and your team. I came into an organization that was thirsting for change and primed for success. Although I was willing to use tried and true leadership principles while employing some unconventional steps to enable the success of our experiment, the bulk of the credit goes to the amazing visionaries that made up portions of my team. Further credit goes to the entire Edwards

Air Force Base workforce that was willing to play an important role in the ultimate test and evaluation of an entire organization and the leader above me, who was massively supportive of the journey. Additionally, key contributions from outside experts in cultural change and design helped craft our roadmap and mold our minds. With our compelling story for context, I will happily share our secrets to success as you read on.

Written by a leader for leaders, this book fuses the ubiquitous topics of leadership and innovation! It powerfully weaves together traditional leadership principles and creative innovation tactics to spur success. Jam-packed with fascinating aviation analogies, little-known stories of Chuck Yeager, intriguing tales from the highest visibility base on the planet, internationally impactful activities in war-torn Iraq, and compelling real-life applications, it takes the reader along on a wildly effective innovation journey while offering a roadmap for replication.

Throughout, you will learn about the foundation of our innovation experience—the *Listen, Consider,* and *Act* cycle. I describe creative methods that include elements we dubbed *Trial by Dragon, Talk with Team Teichert, Dragon's Lair, the Grit Award, the Innovation Manifesto, the Hustle Squad,* and *Charge the Hill.* You will also learn about concepts, like *Spikes on a Wire, Your Calendar and Your Checkbook, Non-Material Solutions, Shared Humanity and Mutual Benefit, Your Greatest Idea,* and *Daring Wins.* As they did for us, these methods can be used to unleash talent and foster an environment of engaged employees in your organization that can help put a major dent in a global $7.8 trillion problem of workforce disengagement and underperformance while also unveiling a distinct opportunity for a massive competitive advantage for you and your organization.

Using these methods, I include details on some of our widespread successes through projects called *Project FoX, Space TPS, C-RAM, IZ Security, Auto-GCAS, Spouse License Portability* and *T-7 Remote Testing.* I also reveal the power of infinite return on investment, psychological moonshots, and targeted boosts to quality of life while emphasizing core leadership concepts that are applicable within and beyond the context of innovation. Finally, I examine the sustainability of an alumni network that fuels an engine of continuing advantage.

Of course, organizational cultural change is a commitment, not a checklist, and progress is never steady nor linear. There will be stumbles, missteps, hardships, and lows. At the insistence of the members of my team, I've also included discussions about these challenges in order to provide a realistic and holistic description of the path to success.

This book acts as a two-for-one resource by wrapping foundational leadership principles into a ground-breaking innovation context for application by anyone, anywhere, in any situation. The turbocharged transformation that results from these methods will quickly make you a believer in the power of unleashing your team and accelerating innovation at supersonic speeds. It is an exciting journey using the unique contexts of jet fuel, Joshua trees and sonic booms that can be applied far beyond the desolate Mojave Desert.

As you light the afterburners of your organization, you will quickly find yourself and your team soaring to new altitudes and airspeeds that will shatter barriers and seize opportunities at the edge of the envelope where no mountain can bury you.

CHAPTER ONE

BREAKING GLASS

On June 21st, 1940, the Muroc Gunnery Range, situated on the edge of a massive dry lakebed on the southwest corner of the sprawling and desolate Mojave Desert about 60 miles north of Los Angeles, was officially activated by the United States Army. Maybe not in miles, but it is a world away from the civilization on the opposite side of the San Gabriel mountains.

Used during the early days by pilots, navigators, and bombardiers to refine their combat skills, it provided the perfect place for final combat checkout before deployment to warfighting theaters in the Pacific and Europe as America entered World War II. Eventually becoming Muroc Army Airfield, military leaders determined that it was the ideal location for the testing of America's first jet-powered aircraft, the P-59 Airacomet.

From its wonderful weather for flight, proximity to the thriving aerospace industry in the Los Angeles area, huge aerial test range over unpopulated areas, and isolation from onlookers to preserve the secrecy of cutting-edge technology, it provided everything a flight test professional would want to perform their important mission. Additionally, those who flew there enjoyed a massive God-made runway complex on a dry lakebed that was as hard as runway concrete and could be used to land in any direction.

Shortly after the United States Air Force became a separate service, Chuck Yeager, a young test pilot and combat hero climbed into the Bell X-1, a rocket-propelled aircraft that looked like a bullet with wings. Launching out of the airfield that would soon be renamed Edwards Air Force Base, he shattered the sound barrier, a limit previously thought of as impossible to break. Flying faster than the speed of sound on that October day in 1947, he expanded the limits of aviation, science, technology, and the human mind.

Chuck Yeager did not start out with a life that telegraphed fame and glory. In fact, as he entered military service slightly before the beginning of World War II, he questioned his ability to rise through the ranks because of his humble West Virginian upbringing and notable lack of formal education. He even got airsick on his first few flights, stumbling through the beginnings of his career! Yet, he pushed forward and went on to serve brilliantly as both a combat and test pilot, and as a leader. In doing so, he broke a slew of aviation records and became known as the quintessential test pilot. Yeager embraced a combination of determination, skill, vision, and grit. Of his historic sound-barrier-breaking flight, he said in his distinct West Virginian drawl, "We didn't know if we could break the sound barrier, but it was our duty to try. That's the way I looked at it."

This spirit has dominated the attitude of test professionals in the Mojave Desert, known by the properly initiated as the Aerospace Valley. Throughout the last 75 years of amazing aviation history, this location has been at the core of nearly every major aerospace milestone.

Fifteen years after Yeager's first supersonic flight and a year after challenging Congress and the nation to "commit itself to achieving the goal, before this decade is out, of landing a man on the Moon and returning him safely to the Earth," President Kennedy addressed a large crowd at the Rice University football stadium in Houston. In his comments to the audience at Rice, he included these powerful thoughts:

CHAPTER ONE ♠ BREAKING GLASS | 13

"But why, some say, the Moon? Why choose this as our goal? And they may well ask, why climb the highest mountain? Why, 35 years ago, fly the Atlantic? Why does Rice play Texas? We choose to go to the Moon! We choose to go to the Moon...We choose to go to the Moon in this decade and do the other things, not because they are easy, but because they are hard; because that goal will serve to organize and measure the best of our energies and skills, because that challenge is one that we are willing to accept, one we are unwilling to postpone, and one we intend to win, and the others, too."

President Kennedy's speech appealed to human nature and instinct. As humans, we are willing to tackle things, in part, because they are hard, and we relish rising to a challenge. We have an innate desire to compete, overcome, and win. With the goal of landing on the moon, humanity tackled something that was hard, and we rose to the challenge. We competed, overcame, and won! We did so in spite of the hard challenges or, maybe, we actually did so by embracing them.

While The Center of the Aerospace Testing Universe is aptly named in its mission to test and evaluate the most innovative technology on the planet, its culture and environment exhibited a strange duality when I arrived in 2018. It was cutting-edge mired in the muck of bureaucracy; an organizational environment characterized by pockets of technical innovation that were stuck in widespread functional stagnation.

Our National Defense Strategy necessitated Edwards be operating at its full capacity and potential. With real international threats on the horizon and a return to a focus on strategic competitors, America's aerospace arsenal was about to be recapitalized. The first flight of the B-21 bomber was just around the corner. Revolutionary unmanned aerial systems, hypersonic weapons, and new fighter, tanker, trainer, and cargo aircraft were on the horizon. Test flights utilizing the novel concepts of autonomy and artificial intelligence were brewing. And yet, the cultural engine at Edwards was stuck in idle.

Prior to arriving at the base as its wing commander, I received a report that had been researched and written by an expensive consulting company, verifying the organizational stagnation. Having assessed the culture and climate at Edwards, it was given the uninspiring innovation grade best described as "Marginal." In every element characterized as a *dimension of innovation,* the organization was given a failing grade, with many of the metrics hovering in the 30% favorable range. Even our standout metric, continuous learning, was rated as a low D at 61%. Our worst rating came in the category that included incentives to innovate.

Essentially, the place charged with propelling America's aerospace arsenal was consumed by a choking complacency when it demanded a thriving culture to match the requirements of its cutting-edge mission. While Harry R. Truman would have been proud, we should have been horrified by our impotence to face the impending technological and strategic eruptions that would bury our defiant and complacent organization. We were on autopilot when we needed to be in afterburner.

As I read the report, the cultural baseline became clear. As negative as the results were, they also illuminated a huge upside awaiting an organization willing to focus on the solutions to a confirmed and verified problem.

Transformation is hard work, and prevailing wisdom suggests it takes years, maybe decades, to adjust an underlying organizational culture. Such challenges, though, didn't stop our test pilot predecessors from breaking barriers and shattering limitations. After all, hard work and a bold vision motivates both literal and figurative moon shots, and I was committed to tearing down the impediments that were stopping true progress at Edwards.

The barriers to real cultural change are high and the challenges onerous. Excuses are easy while solutions are hard. As I considered the significant challenges on our path to cultural change, described below as *Common Barriers to Change,* it became apparent that these were applicable to organizations across a broad spectrum of locations and missions.

COMMON BARRIERS TO CHANGE

Bloated Bureaucracy

Bureaucracies are a wonderful invention of mass production, designed to consistently and repeatably perform a core mission and output their primary deliverable over and over, again and again. Made with multiple layers of specialties to create expertise and economies of scale, they are carefully crafted to centralize decision making authority at the highest possible level in order to minimize risk and maximize success within the environment of the status quo. As a result, they are unable to do anything different as time passes and conditions change.

The generic military is a prime example of a structure of consistency and repeatability. Recruits are trained in a uniform and specific way. New military members start in specialized units at the bottom and follow a slow, plodding path up the chain of command that ultimately rewards loyalty and longevity. Commanders give orders and subordinates follow them: charge the hill, and don't ask why.

This is not unique to military structures. All around us, there are *bloated bureaucracies* or organizations whose processes act like it. The bigger and more established the organization, the more difficult it is for even the most creative among us to imagine a way to circumvent the construct and seize success.

Volumes of Rules and Regulations

Bureaucracies love rules and regulations, seeking out and embracing prescriptive policies and procedures. In the flying world, we say that each new limitation is "written in blood," a reaction to someone's dumb, dangerous, or different action put in place to prevent replication. These guidelines accumulate over time to cover every possible situation, avoid ambiguity and close all loopholes. They are often written in a way that suggests the employee cannot do something unless it is specifically permitted in corporate policy, sapping initiative and draining creativity. They create volumes of limitations, rewarding those who know them best and follow them zealously. These procedures can even be used as weapons by the most ruthlessly ambitious to drag others down whose successful progress is viewed as a threat.

The United States Air Force has its share of rules and regulations, and Airmen are rewarded for abiding by a culture of compliance. For certain things, the rules are important, and following sound processes may make the difference between life and death. After all, you don't want a mechanic unilaterally deciding to omit a bracket on an engine mount because it takes too much time to install correctly. However, since those rules and regulations were not written in stone by the hand of God on Mount Sinai, maybe that mechanic's idea is appropriate for implementation throughout the force, with the appropriate approvals and the right risk assessment, of course.

Not surprisingly, the USAF has a regulation covering the writing and interpretation of regulations—and it is 162 pages long! The rules about rules are so extensive that most people are intimidated by the entire process. And, when it comes to the regulation of regulations, it certainly seems a lot easier to add one than to delete any. In these environments, it is better to simply comply and maintain the course as the robot the bureaucratic designers intended you to be. Regulations were created to eliminate the need for real-time human thinking, and the process to change anything is onerous. Rules simply grow alongside a culture that finds it fruitless to question them.

Exhausting Workload

People are busy in every corner of our society. They are overworked, imbalanced, and burned out, limping towards the next weekend or summer vacation. They are constantly connected and expected to be responsive at all times, even over the weekend or while on vacation! We don't have the hours in the day or the energy in the tank to complete our normal workload. This results in people saying "no" to any activity outside of the norm because they can't seem to find the time or energy to stomach a "yes." The opportunity costs of an *exhausting workload* are job satisfaction, employee engagement, quality of life, and the will to try something different.

Strangling Budgets

A close cousin of *exhausting workload* is *strangling budgets*. More for less is often the expectation in our workplaces, and we are asked to squeeze blood from a turnip. Even if we had time to pursue innovative activity, would we have the financial resources to afford it? How do we justify the investment of precious resources for oblique benefits when those funds could be used to directly fund an immediate priority? It is a lot easier to stick with the traditional, tired, easily explained budgeting lines that produce the same modest results than it is to take a risk with resources that cannot be easily proven to show short-term benefits.

Unreasonable Risk Aversion

It is natural to want to succeed and acceptable for people to be properly recognized for their progress. It is appropriate to want raises, promotions, and awards. In many ways, the system makes clear that the best way to stay on track for those elements of recognition is to maintain the course where you won't be second-guessed. It encourages the focus of one's time, talent, and resources on the easy path where there is no danger to career progression. One mistake can sideline someone on the fast-track to success, and the easiest way to avoid a mistake is to embrace the conservative and convenient comfort of the status quo. To do anything else would require a level of moral courage that often gets eradicated by an organizational culture intent on preserving the system as it is. Thus, *unreasonable risk aversion* is commonplace throughout our societal structures.

Languishing Leadership Inertia

Leaders have grown up in the status quo, enduring and surviving it for years and even decades. More importantly, they have thrived in the status quo. After all, they wouldn't be leaders if they hadn't succeeded in the conditions of past. Why then would they initiate and welcome change when the prevailing rules, regulations, policies and procedures were good enough to get them promoted to leader, commander, boss or CEO?

Long forgotten is the anguish of their times in the trenches. They can easily explain away foolish policies as rites of passage, abusive behavior as character building, inappropriate culture and climate as proud tradition, harsh situations as resiliency-enhancing activities, and inefficiencies as opportunities to prove determination and grit. Someone clamoring for change challenges their entire pathway to success. In their minds, the status quo was good enough for them and should be good enough for those that come after. Thus, the notion of transformation is stifled by *languishing leadership inertia.*

COMMON CHALLENGES INVITE SHARED SOLUTIONS

Bloated bureaucracy, volumes of rules and regulations, exhausting workload, strangling budgets, unreasonable risk aversion, and *languishing leadership inertia* likely all sound familiar. I have seen them in action at every stage of my career. They exist in governments, schools, workplaces, communities, and churches. They even exist in family structures and friend groups. Each of them can suffocate innovation, and all of them together can strangle our innate hope for progress. Unfortunately, they exist in your sphere of influence and realm of impact, making it easy for even the most determined and resilient among us to be fatalistic and pessimistic about our expectations for the future.

These factors weighed on my mind as I drove cross-country towards Edwards Air Force Base in July of 2018, especially while waiting for my cracked windshield to be replaced by a body shop in Las Vegas along the way. I had seen them throughout my career and tried my best to steer organizations away from them. But this time, I wanted to do more than just put band aids on the gaping wounds of stagnant culture and climate.

At Edwards, a place I'd been stationed twice before as a test pilot, I was determined to use my leadership opportunity to do something fundamentally different than anything previously done in the United States Air Force. The needs to do so were substantial and the conditions were ideal. I viewed this as a once-in-a-lifetime opportunity to test and evaluate something beyond what was needed by the military in the air or on orbit. It was time to invest in a wholesale cultural transformation experiment that could fundamentally change our organization. I knew it would be difficult, but tackling hard challenges and breaking glass had yielded some of our society's greatest successes. Now it was our turn!

ACTION ITEM

Action Item 1: Recognize, but do not be deterred, by the Common Barriers to Change. Your organization is not alone in facing these, and you have a chance to break through them. The upside for doing so is massive!

CHAPTER TWO

STREET SIGNS AND QUICK WINS

Chuck Yeager famously quipped, "Never let them name a street after you at Edwards." He expounded on the sacrifice made for revolutionary aviation advances, adding:

"The old-timers at Edwards remembered these guys, but in a couple of years they were just street names out there on the desert. Soon we ran out of streets to name, and in a few very special circumstances, named buildings in honor of outstanding pilots who ran out of luck. Most of them died before they had really made their mark. The real art to test flying was survival; maybe only a spoonful more luck and more skill made the critical difference between a live test pilot and a street name."

After an eight-day drive across our great nation, I arrived at the north gate of Edwards, one of the entrances to this awe-inspiring location with a storied history. Just seeing the street signs powerfully reminded me of the long line of heroism that had created the world-renowned legacy of such a place.

I was first stationed at this legendary location as a Test Pilot School (TPS) student in 2003 as a part of the class known as the Centurions. I was able to stay at Edwards after TPS to test fly the F-22 Raptor in the early days of the program then stationed there again in 2008, first as the Director of Operations then as the Commander of the 411th Flight Test Squadron and Raptor Combined Test Force, responsible for molding and shaping the world's most capable aircraft.

Returning to the base in July of 2018, the opportunity to command such a place took my breath away. It wasn't just the hot temperatures and the high winds; it was the privilege of a lifetime. I proudly snapped a salute to the security forces gate guard and drove past the Joshua Trees onto that sacred ground of flight test and aviation history. I was about to land in a position Chuck Yeager called "the most responsible job in military aviation."

That next day, I took part in a walk-through practice of the change of command ceremony where I would officially accept the responsibility and authority of a commander. I would do so in front of a substantial portion of the organization, and I wanted to set the right tone for my new role, not stumble up the stairs, turn the wrong direction during a movement, or salute at the wrong time. After the practice, I had a few hours with my predecessor to understand the key roles and hot issues awaiting me. While such a meeting is an intimidating whirlwind, I absorbed things that would help make my task and upcoming organizational journey easier to navigate.

In those few hours, I clung to some thoughts that emphasized my belief that I was in the right place at the right time to be a part of a massive organizational cultural transformation experiment.

First, my predecessor had already established a three-person Senior Innovation Council. These leaders were able to provide top-cover for innovators and innovation activity by prioritizing the right innovation efforts and allocating resources to pursue it. Just the creation of such a brain-trust telegraphed to the organization that this was an important effort. I had worked closely with Tony Rubino previously, and I knew that any project he was involved in would be done thoughtfully, thoroughly, and properly. As I got to know Rich Backs and Chris Klug, the other two members of the Senior Innovation Council, it was clear that this was ideal team for such an important purpose.

Second, the previous commander had allocated a notable amount of his organizational budget to invest in innovation activities for the remainder of the year. Not only did this provide amplified priority for such activities, it also gave seed-funds to engage in transformative pursuits. Additionally, I learned that a new cross-cutting organization in the Air Force—AFWERX—was looking for an organization to run the type of a base-wide test that had been on my mind. That support, and the renewed focus on strategic competition in the National Defense Strategy, were all we needed to kick our efforts into high gear in the upcoming months.

The next day was the change of command, and I wanted to leave the wing with a couple of memorable, aspirational statements to provide a common motivational thread throughout my tenure. I wanted the workforce to be inspired, encouraged, and challenged. With an awe-inspiring F-22 Raptor as a backdrop in the same hangar used in the filming of *Captain Marvel* just a few months before, I delivered my speech to an audience filled with prime examples of airpower. And, while I'm not Brie Larson or Samuel L. Jackson, I think my lines hit their mark.

I walked off the stage after the ceremony knowing it was up to me and my incredible team to launch an experiment in cultural change in a world whose eyes were often fixed on what we did in the air, not on the ground.

At the beginning of each new position, I gather my core team to share my leadership philosophy. I do this for a variety of reasons. First, I want my subordinate leaders to get to know me and my leadership style, both for familiarity and accountability purposes. Second, I want them to add to and refine their own leadership philosophy by hearing mine. Third, I want to foster a lifelong leadership journey in these leaders by promoting the journey during my time as commander.

I trust and expect all my teams to hold me accountable for remaining true to the philosophy and style that I claim, and this command was no different. My hope was that my willingness to hear from them would be an indication of a participatory leadership style that would further the transformation I envisioned at Edwards. It was my first allusion to the *listen, consider,* and *act* cycle.

The capstone of my leadership philosophy is a promotion of the potency of servant leadership. Volumes have been written about this concept, and I hesitate to repeat much of that in here.

Several years ago, I read *The Passion of Command: The Moral Imperative of Leadership* by Colonel B.P. McCoy. He was a Marine Battalion Commander during the heaviest fighting in Iraq, and he captured several superb leadership thoughts in his book. On the inside cover, there is an all-caps warning label (as only a Marine would do) that says, "WARNING: WITHOUT GENUINE CONCERN THIS IS ALL WORTHLESS." McCoy is telling the reader to stop reading if they don't have genuine care and concern for their people and the mission. Without it, the reader will be a worthless leader, and I agree!

Servant leadership is not about being soft and friendly or passive and undisciplined. It is also not about forsaking high standards and allowing anything and everything. It's actually quite the opposite! Servant leadership is about embodying and expecting the highest of standards *because you genuinely care.* It is the right thing to do and the most effective way to lead the members of your team to becoming the best possible version of themselves.

Being this type of leader means coupling the enjoyable leadership techniques of inspiration and encouragement with the more difficult techniques of equipping, challenging, and convicting. At times, it also requires employing the unenjoyable leadership technique of correction. To be a servant leader, you must blend these together at the right place, at the right time, in the right situation, with the right people because you genuinely care!

This style creates an environment for human beings to thrive. While helping people become the best possible version of themselves, it also helps the long-term mission of the organization and benefits society by creating other good human beings. I had thrived under a slew of good leaders who employed this style throughout my career, but it wasn't until I recently read another book that I found the best data to prove the potency of such a style.

For my retirement, a friend and former colleague gave me a book called *Do Hard Things: Why We Get Resilience Wrong and the Surprising Science of Real Toughness* by Steve Magness. While devouring the content, a particular paragraph struck me that described the impact of servant leadership on NCAA track teams and the workplace.

The track conclusion was based on a study of athletes from sixty-four teams entitled, "Mental Toughness, Servant Leadership, and the Collegiate Distance Runner." In this study, athletes and teams with servant leader coaches "scored higher on measures of mental toughness and ran faster on the track." The data indicated that performance and resilience were directly enhanced by this type of leadership style. This conclusion was amplified by a study of over a thousand office workers. Having a boss that truly cared ended up being the strongest predictor of work engagement, loyalty, and resilience. The data proved that high performance and a thriving quality of life are both tied directly and substantially to an environment of servant leadership.

As I read the workplace study referenced in Magness's book, I realized something important that I had sensed all along in my leadership experience. Servant leadership and respectful communication isn't primarily about being nice, kind and accommodating. It is actually about creating the right climate and culture through genuine care and concern and employee engagement. "A communicative leader encourages dialogue with employees, shares feedback, and includes employees in decision making."

Such an organization taps into the amazing latent capability of their employees and fully includes them in understanding problems and determining solutions. An organization seizes success in this way by "focusing on inspiring their people and reigniting their workforce," a significant antidote to the global pandemic of disengaged employees that saps productivity and quality of life. Organizations with such a leadership culture enjoy better recruitment and retention, foster higher levels of performance, and achieve greater output and profitability. The results can be staggering!

My plan when assuming my new role was to harness these servant leadership and communication concepts to propel our innovation and transformation journey at The Center of the Aerospace Testing Universe.

The last thing I did during my initial team gathering at Edwards was to pass out notecards and ask my subordinate leaders to jot down some things that I could immediately do to improve our collective ability to care for our people and achieve our mission, a concept I learned from a prior colleague that perfectly aligned with the participatory style described in the workplace study from Magness's book. The submissions could be anonymous if they wanted. This was a way to prime the pump and get them thinking about the long and bold journey they would join me on in the days, weeks, and months to follow.

As I read through the inputs provided by my team, it became clear that these improvements were just the tip of the iceberg. Easy changes to processes, waivers to policy, and delegation of authority could yield big results. With quick wins and public follow-through, this path would set the stage for our journey ahead and begin a cycle of *listening, considering,* and *acting.*

At the end of my first day, I headed to meet my family for dinner, driving off base on the roads whose names rang out with memories of history and valor, and each glance was a poignant reminder of the weighty responsibility of my new job.

ACTION ITEMS

Action Item 1: Utilize aspirational phrases to give your workforce a sense of pride and responsibility about who they are, what they do, and how they contribute to something important.

Action Item 2: Employ a servant leadership style to unlock the full talent of your team.

Action Item 3: Create a culture and climate of respectful communication.

Action Item 4: Find ways to easily demonstrate the intent of your participatory leadership style and quickly and publicly follow-through on suggestions to ignite positive progress

CHAPTER THREE

UNLEASHING THE TEAM

Edwards' long and storied history is known for its maverick pilots. These renegades liked thrills and, more importantly, had a passion for meaningful results, free from restrictive rules and regulations. Some would call them crazy, but their craziness had produced countless innovative milestones that shaped the course of recent human history. One of the most extravagant of these mavericks wasn't a pilot, but a physician.

Dr. John Stapp was an Air Force officer, physicist, and flight surgeon. Over his impressive career, he played a primary role in improving the safety equipment for pilots, with inventions including safety harnesses and ejection equipment. Stapp performed his important role in the deserts of California and New Mexico using a unique piece of test equipment called a *rocket sled*, a contraption made of a rocket-engine-propelled sled on rail tracks. It was used to test the effects of powerful acceleration, high-speed wind blast, and rapid decelerations on the human body.

Before highly instrumented test dummies were invented, human test dummies rode the sled, with Stapp insisting that he be in the seat for the most extreme and dangerous conditions. As a result, he shattered bones, broke ribs, and faced temporary blindness—all for the cause of science and pilot safety.

In performing these tests, Stapp became known as "the fastest man on earth," breaking land speed records while strapped to a rocket. Yet, his craziness had an important purpose, and the safety mechanisms on aircraft improved significantly under his carefully crafted rocket sled test plans. He even invented the three-point safety belt system, the forerunner to modern day seat belts used in all vehicles around the world. Stapp, in the spirit of Murphy's Law—"anything that can go wrong, will go wrong"—made an impact on all of humanity through his unleashed and unorthodox methods.

I excitedly settled into my role and enjoyed catching frequent glimpses of aircraft out my office window. It was an airshow every day at The Center of the Aerospace Testing Universe. They even let me fly on occasion, and, for the third time in my career, I got checked out to fly the F-22 Raptor. While the aircraft were impressive, the team at Edwards was incredible. They were the true national treasure that resided in this corner of the Mojave Desert. The team seemed primed and ready for a journey to the edge of the innovation and organizational transformation envelope.

The leadership team scheduled a strategic offsite for us in Palmdale a few weeks into my new position. The place was simply called Plant 42, but it was here where much of the world-changing aerospace capabilities had been developed over the past several decades. Edwards is ultimately responsible for the operation of the sprawling industrial location there that hosts the cutting-edge activities of aerospace giants, like Northrup and Boeing, and the headquarters of the famed Lockheed Skunk Works. They would design and build it, and we would fly, test, and evaluate it at Edwards. This offsite location was another perfect reminder of the revolutionary work that required an organization with the ability to operate at the speed of relevance. I was ready to see how we could commit to a bold path with buy-in from the senior leaders at such an event.

As I drove to Plant 42, I recounted my recent briefing on Edwards' role in testing a series of upcoming hypersonic weapons that would fly faster than five times the speed of sound. The Russians and Chinese had been recently rumored to already have such capability in their operational forces, and America was behind. I couldn't figure out how we'd flown the X-15, an icon of aviation that exceeded *six times* the speed of sound as a manned aircraft in 1961, yet were struggling, nearly 60 years later, to create a much smaller, unmanned weapon that would go that fast. I couldn't quite reconcile the disconnect, likely caused in part by societal stagnation and risk aversion that had crept into our cultural psyche since then, but I was determined to do what I could to move our organization beyond the limitations that harmed our national pride and hindered our national pursuits.

I officially began the offsite with my understanding of the gripping thoughts contained in the newly released National Defense Strategy. We then assessed our organizational strengths, weaknesses, opportunities, and threats, and established strategic initiatives to hold ourselves accountable as signs of real progress based on the results of our analysis.

We agreed to strive to "Accelerate Innovation" as one of our five priorities, but we struggled to find the right verb to use as we looked to fully unlock the talent, energy, attention, and passion of our workforce. Words matter, and our discussion demonstrated a duality of risk tolerance levels among the members of our senior leadership team.

It was already apparent during the discussion that some of our senior leaders were less than eager to fully embrace the pursuit of innovation. There was concern that we were innovating for the sake of innovation. Some had seen failed attempts at creating a culture of innovation when incentives and priorities had been misaligned. Many were intimidated by the consultant's report that indicated how far away we were from truly being an innovative organization. A handful were satisfied with being better than average.

FLASHBACK TO MIT (1990)

During my freshman year in college, I took a C-programming course. The weekly homework assignments were based on writing code and typically took 20 hours to complete. It was hard! I picked up the material fairly quickly but was still far from mastering the content.

I knew I had bombed a particular test even as I turned it in. When I received my grade, a miserable 29 percent, I noticed the letter A next to it and was confused. The professor explained that, while I'd only gotten 29% correct, I was sufficiently better than class average, which translated to an A. So, fortunately for me, my classmates were greater failures than I! It was on that day that I learned a lesson more important than the course content: You can still be horrible even though you are better than average.

As I sat in that offsite, I realized that some had complacently settled on being better than average. Something had to be done!

As we dissected this topic, several members of the team liked the more "industrial age" terms, such as *encouraging, equipping, or challenging* the workforce. Other members offered up more "progressive" phrasing, like *unleashing* or *unshackling* the workforce. A debate ensued. The more conservative leaders were worried about such radical words, thinking that they would encourage a disregard for common practices, acceptable policies, and trusted regulations. They feared our workforce would latch onto such thoughts in a dangerous and costly way. Those who liked the more aggressive words acknowledged their provocative nature but also understood the need to prod behavior through a change in terminology that accepted more risk. They needed the workforce to accept the intent of these terms without reckless behavior. It came down to an exercise in trust. Fortunately, I'd been through a similar situation that I could draw on to best lead my team in the right direction.

FLASHBACK TO JOINT BASE ANDREWS (2016-2018)

As a commander at multiple levels, I knew the importance of stewardship and mission success. During my previous assignment at Joint Base Andrews from 2016-2018, a number of distinguished

CHAPTER THREE ♣ **UNLEASHING THE TEAM** | 33

visitors had traversed its flight line, making it essential for every member of the team to be acting at their highest capability. The diverse grouping of high-priority missions made it difficult to be everywhere at once, so I had to trust my team.

At a normal base, you could shut down routine operations to prepare for a VIP delegation. At Andrews, the VIP load was so high and so frequent that four-star generals and even the Vice President of the United States were regarded as a part of the baseline routine since the President and foreign heads of state regularly utilized the base.

Missions from Andrews also included the constant posture required to launch F-16s to intercept potential threats approaching the D.C. area, an air-to-air tanker force considered part of major operational plans, a communication backbone to maintain connection between the Commander-in-Chief and Executive Branch anywhere on the planet, a helicopter force on 24-hour alert in the case of a national emergency, and a golf course offering stress relief for the President.

To succeed in such a demanding environment, there is no option but to trust the entirety of your force. The importance of this proved most powerful during the 70th birthday of the United States Air Force in September 2017.

The Air Force Chief of Staff had directed each Major Command (a headquarters with a slew of bases under their authority) to execute a high-level birthday event during that calendar year. As the schedule came together, Joint Base Andrews was responsible for *three* such events in a single 20-hour period while other, multi-base commands were required to do just one event at some point in the year. The order was tall, but I knew we were up to the task!

Our teams came together and developed a schedule, which began on a Thursday evening with the United States Air Force Tattoo—a ceremony event that included a rock concert, parade, flyovers, fireworks, and high-level speeches. On Friday morning, the base would host the opening-day of a three-day airshow, the first in a decade, where tens of thousands of visitors would descend upon the

> base to enjoy a superb demonstration of airpower. On that same day, the President would arrive on base to tour facilities and be briefed on a range of Air Force capabilities. Additionally, he would give an internationally televised live speech congratulating the Air Force on its birthday before departing to Mar-a-Lago for the weekend.
>
> There were not enough higher-ranking leaders to oversee the preparation and execution activities for this slate of events. But we didn't need them! We simply had to trust our people to execute our intent and use their judgment. And they did so brilliantly!

In spite of the debate at the offsite, the conservative senior leader crowd eventually became comfortable with the more provocative expressions they originally hesitated to support. As a result, we were able to agree upon a phrase to express our vision that combined the newer and traditional terms. We were going to *Develop, Inspire, and Unleash our Total Force.* The leaders signed their names to our strategic plan, which included this phrase and was to be distributed to the entirety of our organization. We were ready to launch our campaign!

Our first priority was to define what we meant by innovation. We needed to be sure it wasn't perceived as a superficial, fancy new process or flashy program. We didn't want it to be a hollow talking point from a boss to give us empty comfort in our progress. It was to be viewed as far more than pointless innovation theater.

Our vision was real and intended to be mission-enhancing and cross-cutting. It needed to be a financially reasonable rallying-point for our entire base. However, it also shouldn't distract us from our overall mission or drain us of our scarce resources. We wanted the totality of the base to become an innovation laboratory, so we proposed something simple.

Any member of our team with an idea needed to know that someone in leadership would *listen* to it, *consider* it, and *act* appropriately on it. Even if we didn't get to yes, our simple acts of *listening, considering* and *acting* would allow us to tap into the talent all around us, snapping the workforce out of autopilot and unleashing our team.

For this to work, we needed to convince the base population that we were open to *listening,* willing to *consider* their ideas and committed to following through with the appropriate *action.* The notecard exercise used during my day-one leadership philosophy was a good start, but this concept couldn't be confined to the leadership team. It needed to spread to every member of the organization. So, drawing from my previous leadership experiences, we launched a concept called *Dragon's Lair* that produced tangible results.

FLASHBACK TO ROYAL AIR FORCE LAKENHEATH (1998)

In the fighter-pilot world, fliers give one another call signs. These are bestowed during a big squadron ceremony early on in a flier's first operational assignment. The names generally sound cool but are mostly based on a stupid act or personal characteristic. The first few months typically provide enough opportunities for new-guy or new-gal buffoonery to create a portfolio of options. I was happy to get named Dragon, though its origin, stemming from Zaragoza, Spain and nuclear weapons, was far from glamorous and will not be shared here.

Yet, because dragons gather treasure in their lairs, it seemed fitting for me to gather the treasure of great ideas in an online forum given the same name. So, I set out to develop an old-school suggestion box with a 21st Century touch and Dragon's Lair was born.

My team had several new engineers waiting for security clearances that were stuck in the painfully-long bureaucratic approval process. They had done all the training possible in an unclassified environment to prepare for their eventual roles and were looking to put their talents to good use while they waited. Creating a base-wide app seemed like the perfect task, so I proposed it to them, and they were thrilled to be given such a responsibility.

The easy-to-use app provided a slew of important information, like maps, schedules, weather conditions, services, and activities, for our base population. Anonymous questions, concerns, critiques, compliments, ideas, and recommendations could be typed into the Dragon's Lair portion of the app from the convenience of a phone. The input would then be directly emailed to me, without any filtering or editing. After listening to and considering the information then discussing it with the experts on my team, I would take action by responding. However, since these inputs were anonymous, my reply went to the entire base population!

To foster transparency and a cohesive team environment, we purposely designed the app to allow the entire base population to see every input sent to me and each associated response. I needed to prove that I was serious about this concept of *listen, consider,* and *act,* and, because of the app, the base population noticed.

Inputs started slow, as people determined my commitment to it, but participation ramped up quickly. After a short time, I was receiving around a dozen inputs a week and personally responding to every single one. While some were hard truths wrapped in less-respectful language than I preferred and others a bit unexpected (like the suggestion for the entire base to start each day with group yoga), all were important and all were needed.

Each one got my personal attention to *listen, consider,* and *act* appropriately. Sometimes, my action was to reply that the idea was neither feasible nor wise, but my response always included a thorough explanation outlining my rationale. I made sure to follow through with the viable ideas to show that my replies were not the only action. I would engage the team to implement these ideas and publicize it when we did so.

Through the Dragon's Lair experience, we learned that military spouses were having difficulty finding employment on and off base, so we stood up a spouse hiring program and initiated a spouse job fair. We uncovered shared concerns that general parking spaces were being monopolized by the amount of reserved parking spots on base, so we assessed the situation and reduced the number of the reserved spots to accommodate. Inputs received about the lack of cell phone coverage prompted us to initiate a project to erect two new cell towers. These are just a few examples of the impact of Dragon's Lair.

To promote the commitment to the *listen, consider, act* philosophy, we did our best to publicize these wins, which often meant me traveling to a pertinent location around base and filming short videos, which proved worthwhile. My team even bought me a gyro-stabilized selfie-stick to prevent the shaking responsible for the motion sickness people initially got while watching the videos. My family mocked my selfie technology, but that was a small price to pay to see the base population respond and begin believing that we were serious in the *listen, consider,* and *act* cycle.

Dragon's Lair became a formalized process that reinforced one of my favorite conversation starters as I walked around our installation. In nearly every conversation, I would weave in three key questions to further reinforce that we were *listening, considering,* and *acting.*

- What am I doing wrong?
- What are we doing wrong?
- What can I do to help?

Word soon spread that we were serious, and our reputation for follow-through was a key component of our progress. I saw positive movement in every input and response as we started to unleash our world-class team through the *listen, consider* and *act* cycle. We weren't striving to be test-dummy mavericks like Dr. Stapp, but we did want to doggedly find ways to remove the obstacles hindering progress.

ACTION ITEMS

Action Item 1: Words matter—commit to using words that are as bold as your organizational vision.

Action Item 2: Once you communicate your intent effectively, trust your team to follow it.

Action Item 3: Creating a culture of innovation is not about a single, flashy idea. Unleash your team by listening, considering, and acting.

Action Item 4: Create various forums to solicit ideas and feedback from your team.

Action Item 5: Aggressively and publicly follow-up on the ideas you receive from your team.

CHAPTER FOUR

SUFFICIENT RUNWAY

Pancho Barnes was a ground-breaking pilot and a fixture among the Hollywood elite in the 1940s and 50s. She was also an eccentric mainstay of the Edwards Air Force Base community, owning property just to the west of the original base contours. Her roadhouse restaurant and bar was a popular hangout for the likes of Chuck Yeager and his colleagues. Her property eventually expanded into a large dude ranch that included a motel, swimming pool, and airstrip to cater to her aviation clientele from Los Angeles and beyond who came to attend her legendary parties. Yet, in 1954, her property was consumed in a hostile takeover by a growing base.

At the time, the nation was considering the creation of a nuclear-powered bomber aircraft, which could fly indefinitely without the need for traditional fuel. Such a concept required an aircraft capable of carrying a very heavy nuclear reactor, and such a massive aircraft required an excessively long runway to takeoff. Even the existing 15,000-foot runway at Edwards wasn't long enough to get such an aircraft airborne, so the base started buying land to the west of its existing property.

Pancho's property stood in the way of the government plans, so they seized her land, ending an era and crushing the booming business of a successful entrepreneur. Sadly, the nuclear-powered aircraft concept was never actually created, but the idea that an aircraft could fly indefinitely continues to be an attractive consideration. It would just need a sufficiently long runway to get started on its mission. Anything less wouldn't do.

I got fired up as we rolled out our strategic plan to our workforce and began using phrases about accelerating innovation and unleashing our team. I knew we were on the precipice of something magnificent that would fundamentally change our organization and trigger others to follow in our footsteps. I was ready to get started in a wholesale way with a short takeoff launch. As far as I was concerned, the conditions were ideal, and we had the right tools at our disposal. However, the plodding military bureaucracy is a quintessential example of a slow system, and, unfortunately, patience isn't always my strong suit.

FLASHBACK TO SEYMOUR JOHNSON AFB (2001)

My personal impatience with military bureaucratic latency peaked in 2001. I arrived at Seymour Johnson Air Force Base, North Carolina from my first operational assignment at Royal Air Force Lakenheath, United Kingdom, flying F-15E Strike Eagles. I had qualified as an instructor during that first tour and had been assigned as an instructor for new F-15E pilots and weapon system officers (WSOs) in this new unit.

To become an instructor at my new assignment, though, there was an extensive checkout program. While it is a bit ridiculous to need to checkout as an instructor when you were already a current and qualified instructor, the rationale revolved around the differences between being an operational-unit instructor and training-unit instructor. There was a small cadre of new instructors in my same situation, and we endured the same silliness together.

It wouldn't have been a big deal if the checkout process were streamlined or if the unit prioritized our checkout to finish quickly.

Unfortunately, neither of those situations played out in our favor, and the process was long and onerous. The unit was behind in its training of the new student pilots and WSOs and decided to not let us even start the instructor checkout process until they were caught up with the current schedule. We asked to return to our old units and were told no. We asked to go across the street to a different operational unit to keep current in our flying skills and were told no. We asked to go to some mandatory non-flying training as we waited and were told no. So, we sat and sat and sat and sat. It was a waste of useful and motivated manpower. Needless to say, we grew a bit salty in the process.

On the day that our instructor course exceeded the duration of our original checkout, I was fed up. It was taking longer to get checked out as an instructor when we were already instructors than it was to learn how to fly and employ the Strike Eagle when we had started with zero experience. Though I was just a Captain, I thought we should wage a protest in the best way possible in a community that recognized the power of ridicule and sarcasm.

A la David Letterman, I created a Top 10 list of things that had been accomplished in less time than it took to complete the 333rd Fighter Squadron Lancer Instructor Course. Our leaders were not amused, but the experience was cathartic. The list included.

- The journey to discover the New World—It only took Christopher Columbus 226 days to reach the Americas and return home to Spain.
- The conquering of mainland Europe by Allied Forces during World War II—The Allies took 291 days from the invasion at Normandy until they crossed the Rhine River.
- The creation of the U.S. Constitution—It took for our Founding Fathers 116 days consider, debate, and write the U.S. Constitution in the summertime heat in Philadelphia, Pennsylvania in 1787.

In September of 2018, I introduced the 116-Day Innovation Blitz, a name with a nod to both football, since that season had just begun, and the signing of the U.S. Constitution, as its anniversary was on the horizon. I thought it would be encouraging to cite a time when the world saw an innovation of government unmatched in human history. Imagine, 116 days in the summertime heat in Philadelphia, Pennsylvania in 1787 without modern conveniences and yet they got it done! What could possibly be our excuse?

In my excitement about our bold journey, I began publicly broadcasting about our Innovation Blitz, crafting my own talking points and writing my own press releases. The following is an example of what I started to push out to the team.

"For the next 116 days, we will aggressively follow our forefathers' lead. We are instituting an innovation blitz in every unit and throughout our wing. We will leverage all of the energy and creativity that we can muster to pursue those innovations that will improve our processes, our lives, our units, and our ability to test and evaluate for the warfighter. We will look within ourselves, and we will look around us. We will collaborate with others in the test community and throughout the Aerospace Valley.

In less than four months, our founders scrapped the government that enabled victory in the Revolutionary War in order to create something that was magnificent and lasting. What can we do over the next few months that is magnificent and lasting at The Center of the Aerospace Testing Universe? Our nation needs us to figure this out together, and I look forward to being dazzled by the full-scale 116-Day Innovation Blitz of our world-class team."

While the words sounded great, I hadn't fully considered whether we could actually harness this creativity and construct a foundation for our cultural transformation. I found out rather quickly that *we could not*. Fortunately, it wasn't too late.

Shortly after I started talking about my idea, our Senior Innovation Council scheduled a meeting with me. Tony, Chris, and Rich had some real concerns, and, because Tony knew me best, he broke the news.

While they loved the general concept of the Innovation Blitz, Tony tactfully explained that there were some major hurdles, preventing it from creating opportunity and meeting its full potential. Primarily, there was not yet the structure of people, processes and systems to absorb the onslaught of ideas that might flow from such a campaign. We needed a way to capture these, then input, mature, prioritize, fund, and act on them. Without the manpower, financing, computer mechanism, and process structure, these ideas would be lost or languished. Momentum would fizzle.

Once I absorbed and understood the concerns of the Senior Innovation Council, I was grateful for their courage in speaking up. I realized they were not trying to slow me down or dampen my enthusiasm. They were simply ensuring we had a deliberate and sustainable plan and path forward. They were also guaranteeing that we properly parlayed our earlier momentum into our one big chance to establish and maintain credibility when it came to a commitment for cultural transformation. Based on their counsel, we modified the 116-Day Innovation Blitz.

At this point, we needed the members of our team to cultivate ideas and engage in discussions. The Blitz was the period where innovation would germinate, ending with the launch of a full-blown campaign ready to absorb all the great ideas brewing during the 116 days.

The result was a successful Blitz, but only because it was molded by a leadership team that prevented us from squandering a singular opportunity for progress. Similar to a nuclear-powered bomber aircraft that required sufficient runway for its takeoff roll, we needed the right amount of runway for our sustainable cycle of *listening, considering,* and *acting*. We must not rush into the air without the appropriate organizational airspeed.

ACTION ITEMS

Action Item 1: Obtain buy-in and perspective from your senior leaders and fully consider the pathways and processes for success before making decisions about a major leadership initiative. Don't accept slow processes, but restrain your haste in order to do things well instead of doing things quickly and poorly.

Action Item 2: Establish a reliable and sustainable way to capture ideas, input, mature, prioritize, fund, and act on them as a part of the *listen, consider,* and *act* cycle.

CHAPTER FIVE

YOUR CALENDAR AND YOUR CHECKBOOK

The SR-71 Blackbird was a miracle of aviation prowess crafted by the famed Lockheed Skunk Works. Built and originally flown in the 1960s, it could blatantly fly over heavily defended enemy territory using its exceedingly high operating altitude and blazing speed to outrun any supersonic surface-to-air missile that would try to bring it down. Those enemy weapons would be left in the dust by the Blackbird as it snapped pictures and gathered highly-sought-after intelligence from directly over the homeland of an adversary. One was never brought down by an enemy, and it was eventually retired as a NASA research aircraft in 1999.

Interestingly, it was originally named the RS-71 Blackbird, using the naming convention of the day to emphasize the long-range Reconnaissance mission of this amazing aircraft. Yet, in the announcement of the aircraft to the public, President Lyndon Baines Johnson accidentally reversed the letters and called it the SR-71. Rather than acknowledging the simple error in the speech, the Air Force renamed it and forced the contractor to update over 29,000 manuals, blueprints, and drawings. It was a costly decision that abided by rigid hierarchy instead of common sense.

In preventing my unforced error in the Innovation Blitz, the Senior Innovation Council saved the day by highlighting common sense instead of rigid hierarchy. Yet, our arsenal still lacked a crucial component that we needed before we were truly ready for the full-blown campaign starting at the end of the 116-day cultivation period. The idea for this next stage came from Tony, Chris, and Rich, and it proved to be the most pivotal decision in this part of our journey.

This group of core innovation leaders wisely recognized the need for a younger team to ignite the campaign in a way that could only arise through a bottom-up surge of energy and enthusiasm. Additionally, they identified the need for dedicated manpower to manage a campaign that we expected to be popular and robust.

Innovation cannot be directed via a tasker process nor through a senior leader edict. It cannot flow from a talking point or through centralized control. This will simply generate superficial activity instead of targeted transformation. Instead, innovation needs to bubble up organically and passionately from the wellspring of the workforce and stem from the heart and soul of the organization. An *American Psychologist* article coined this concept, "The Power of Self-Persuasion."

"In contrast with traditional, direct techniques of persuasion (advertising, political rhetoric, etc.), self-persuasion is indirect and entails placing people in situations where they are motivated to persuade themselves to change their own attitudes or behaviors. We find that where important attitudes, behavior, or lifestyle changes are concerned, self-persuasion strategies produce more powerful and longer-lasting effects than do direct techniques of persuasion. This is primarily due to the fact that members of an audience are constantly aware of the fact that someone is trying (or has tried) to influence them in direct persuasion. In a self-persuasion situation, people are convinced that the motivation for change comes from within."

Please don't misunderstand me here, there is a necessary role for the senior leader to trigger and protect this up swell of activity, but it is not sufficient for true success. Firm direction of a leader is akin to the traditional, direct forms of persuasion that are often resisted by subordinates. On the other hand, peer-coaxed persuasion is more easily

CHAPTER FIVE ♣ YOUR CALENDAR AND YOUR CHECKBOOK | 47

absorbed as a component of self-persuasion. Recognizing this, the *Hustle Squad* at Edwards was born.

We called for manpower to form this small but critical team. It wasn't an additional duty, but more like a full-time rotating position that would form the core of our cultural change movement. It required the most competent and compassionate members of our organization to ensure it was done right. This team would form the structure around which all base-wide innovation activity would coalesce. Most importantly, they would reflect the best of our organization and foster a contagious bottom-up cultural change movement.

The members of the Hustle Squad came from organizations that spanned our mission set, originating from diverse backgrounds that accurately reflected our population and were relatively young yet accomplished. They had technical skills and relational talents. As I got to know them, I called them the *Cool Kids* because they had an aurora of charisma and swagger that I hoped would catch on throughout the organization. As I watched these superstars perform their important role and observed their remarkable successors do the same, I witnessed a personification of our entire cultural innovation journey. In my mind, these individuals were the actual icons of innovation.

The Hustle Squad formed, bonded, and got right to work. They created their name from our desire to overcome the natural latency in our prevailing processes, matching our need to act at the speed of relevance. We found office space for the team in the basement of our dining facility, and, while it was initially sparse, they quickly turned it into a launching pad for a journey of maximum thrust. Not only were they a potent group of influencers, just the act of our investment in full-time innovation activity was a powerful sign of our commitment to this effort.

The team lead, Heidi Williams, had been recruited from cutting-edge efforts in emerging technologies, including autonomy, artificial intelligence, and counter-unmanned aerial system weapons to protect our nation's bases from adversary drones. She was a skilled flight test engineer with a passion for cultural change and a natural fit for innovation-fueled leadership. She had started her working life as a journalist with an inclination to buck the status quo. Her Hustle Squad colleagues, though some were a bit more traditional in their perspectives, came from similar high-visibility, high-impact areas, yielding a creative tension that ultimately produced rich brainstorming sessions along with some angst. By taking a bit of manning risk in our traditional mission areas, we were intentionally highlighting something more fundamentally crucial to our long-term successes—innovation and organizational transformation.

Alongside their cultural horsepower, the Hustle Squad also provided practical elements to our journey, as they were ultimately responsible for absorbing all the recommendations from our team during the upcoming campaign. Based on our preparatory activities, we expected a tidal wave of inputs that needed to be captured, input, matured, prioritized, funded and acted on. In order to handle the anticipated magnitude of ideas, the Hustle Squad needed to create and publicize the online structure and automated processes that would absorb and follow through on all inputs. Thus, they were to shape the scaffold upon which we would incorporate the ideas from our broader workforce.

However, the Hustle Squad wasn't expected to do so alone. They enlisted a volunteer force to fully man the campaign, with the most eager and engaged becoming key members of the follow-on Hustle Squad generation to make it a self-perpetuating activity. They jumped in with both feet, exciting the rest of the force for what was just around the corner.

I regularly met with the Hustle Squad, offering my support and vision to guide their activity. I also provided the necessary resources to plug in the afterburners during our organizational journey. Initially, I met with them to provide inspiration but quickly discovered that it was I who walked away from every engagement inspired and encouraged.

With each interaction, they gained confidence in and understanding of the boldness of our objective while I felt more comfortable setting them loose to achieve it. I felt like General Dwight D. Eisenhower when he said, "A commander meets to talk to his men to inspire them. With me it's the other way around. I get inspired by you." Additionally, as the

Edwards community saw our connection, they further understood the priority of these efforts and sensed the inspiration I was feeling.

In speaking about the unique culture of Herb Kelleher's Southwest Airlines, authors Kevin and Jackie Frieberg make the powerful statement in their book *Nuts*.

"If we wanted to learn more about your values, we would ask to see two things: your checkbook and your calendar. How you spend your money and your time tells us a lot about what you value. The same is true for organizations. Employees, consciously or not, learn about an organization's values by watching how the company and its executives spend company money and use company time."

A workforce knows what their leaders value and prioritize by what they do with their resources, not by what they say. Therefore, I met with the Hustle Squad frequently and supported them fully, liberally demonstrating the value of their efforts through my finances and my time—by my checkbook and my calendar. I did my best to avoid hindering their leadership of these critical efforts because our success could only come from fully supporting them to ignite bottom-up activity.

Leadership sets the tone for the culture and climate of an organization. While a cultural change cannot be driven by top-down direction, it can and must be protected by senior leaders. Otherwise, innovators and revolutionaries will likely be squashed by those wedded to the comforts of the status quo. With the Hustle Squad and the rest of our transformation efforts, it was the responsibility of the Senior Innovation Council and me to guide, support, and protect Heidi and her team. Such a leadership philosophy is also a key component of an organization that achieves mission success and boosts quality of life.

FLASHBACK TO EDWARDS AFB (2011)

When I was the squadron commander of the F-22 test organization at Edwards earlier in my career, I was asked to write a leadership article for the base paper. I thought deeply about the subject of my article and concluded that time management principles would be most relevant to every reader. After all, there is nothing more egalitarian than time. Everyone has the exact same amount of it, and success is ultimately based on how well an individual or organization uses it.

At that time, the F-22 was in the midst of the biggest modernization program in its history. Our organization was given a very short timeline to test and evaluate a slew of new capabilities to add to an aircraft designed to dominate in air-to-air engagements. This included advanced air-to-ground capability, allowing us to also provide lethal capabilities against ground targets while the aircraft was moving much faster than the speed of sound. It was a challenging test environment and one that required the best possible time management to complete our weighty responsibilities without burning out our incredible team. This was the challenge I drew from while writing my article, "Our Most Precious Resource."

I explained that leaders engaging in activity that can be accomplished by others is an unwise use of their time that comes with a massive opportunity cost. "Proper prioritization is the key to budgeting our time properly, and such prioritization does not happen by accident. It takes thought, reflection, and assessment." Without clear priorities, "it is easy to be enslaved by our often meaningless 'to do' lists or the next flashy task that passes our way ... our priorities should structure and triage our tasks so that the tasks themselves don't become priorities by default."

When leaders spend time doing anything other than those things that they can uniquely accomplish it "stifles initiative and hinders growth." A leader, especially one who wants to guide their

CHAPTER FIVE ♣ **YOUR CALENDAR AND YOUR CHECKBOOK** | 51

organization into a future of innovation and transformation, needs to focus on a few primary things to realize success.

- Serving and Supporting People
- Building Relationships
- Casting A Bold and Compelling Vision
- Setting Broad Limits in The Pursuit of That Vision
- Appropriately Resourcing the Achievement of That Vision
- Breaking Down Barriers That Hinder a Workforce and Block Achievement of That Vision
- Getting Out of The Way

As a wing commander at that same location several years later, I carefully considered how I structured and telegraphed my priorities. I was mindful of our F-22 successes as a squadron commander. I was also constantly cognizant about what I was telling our team through my actions and the deliberate utilization of my calendar and checkbook. In my engagement with a hugely capable Hustle Squad, these things were constantly at the forefront of my mind. I always wanted to focus on common sense instead of rigid hierarchy, unlike the flail that resulted from President Johnson's misspeak at the unveiling of the RS-71 Blackbird.

ACTION ITEMS

Action Item 1: Structure your organization's innovation journey through bottom-up enthusiasm, not top-down direction.

Action Item 2: Commit manpower and finances in order to foster innovation and encourage young innovators.

Action Item 3: Prioritize your calendar and checkbook to transmit your priorities.

Action Item 4: Only engage in those activities that you can uniquely accomplish.

CHAPTER SIX

CHARGING THE HILL

On December 17th, 1777, two-and-a-half years into the American Revolutionary war, General George Washington and his American Continental Army arrived at Valley Forge. They faced brutal conditions, and their ability to withstand that environment for the next several months would determine the ultimate success of the American revolutionary cause. Things were desperate and hope was dwindling.

On the day of their arrival at Valley Forge, General Washington published a brilliant two paragraph General Order to be read to the approximate 12,000 soldiers there in the cold and dreary environment in Pennsylvania. The first paragraph oozes with leadership lessons that include the potency of motivation and purpose, the power of explanatory communications, and the prestige of selfless servant leadership. The second paragraph, though, had a different message, a focus on the importance of community.

General Washington and his soldiers had a lot to do as they settled into their new winter home. They needed clothes, shelter, shoes, food, fuel, and weapons. After all, the camp was characterized by bloody footprints on the snow because of their lack of basic necessities. Yet, on their first full day in the camp, Washington directed these soldiers to focus on building community. His powerful call to prioritize prayer and worship, while rich with spiritual significance, carried relational significance as well. These hardened soldiers would need God and one another to make it through the harsh conditions of the next several months. Washington knew that the revolutionary success required the bonds of trust and togetherness that could only develop through an intentional focus on activities that would foster such critical characteristics.

As the Hustle Squad quickly adjusted to their new role, we found an opportunity to grow in our mutual understanding of our collective mission and one another. Through my amazing Senior Enlisted Leader, Command Chief Roosevelt "RJ" Jones, we had heard of a ground-breaking innovative organization in the United States Air Force that was several hours north of us near Sacramento, California.

Beale Air Force Base, home of the U-2 Dragon Lady, had an intelligence group that had earned a reputation for its ground-breaking innovative culture. While that culture had not scaled up to the base-wide level, innovation at this scale could be informative to our journey. Thus, we decided to take a road trip together as a community-building activity to develop ties with other likeminded innovators.

There was a huge fringe benefit to such a trip. Chief Jones was approaching the end of his tenure, and losing someone of his caliber in the midst of our innovation journey would be devastating if I could not find the right replacement. Therefore, I needed to start the search and hiring process soon and would leave no stone unturned. It is an absolutely critical decision for a Wing Commander to pick his key wingman, and I had been spoiled by Chief Jones at Edwards and Chief Nate Perry at Joint Base Andrews. I wanted to get this decision right to maintain my streak of model partnership between officer and enlisted leaders at the Command Team level.

Chief Ian Eishen was the Senior Enlisted Leader of the intelligence group we would visit at Beale. He was known as an innovation and transformation juggernaut, a force of nature who could just as easily rub shoulders with junior members of the force, senior leaders of the service, and the educational and technological titans of Silicon Valley that found ways to collaborate with the intelligence group. Not only would our trip north allow me to learn from his innovation journey, it would also give me the time to size him up as a possibility to be my next Command Chief. Thus, and unbeknownst to him, our visit to Beale doubled as an all-day job interview.

As we chatted with Chief Eishen and the members of the team at Beale, our team from Edwards was encouraged by our planned path forward. We saw a group-level organization not just performing innovation theater but pursuing, embracing and achieving true cultural transformation. We asked a lot of questions, watched them in action, and took a ton of notes. The most powerful point-to-ponder came from Chief Eishen about the allocation of resources to best achieve long-lasting innovation activity. He contended that the best use of resources was to find opportunities to educate the members of the workforce who were eager to become innovation leaders.

Chief Eishen's rationale was simple, a leader might invest a certain amount of money in pursuit of a single innovative solution. In that case, a solution would yield a singular success. As an alternative, a leader could invest the same amount of money in providing innovation-related educational opportunities to several members of the workforce. In that case, those innovation team members would be equipped to solve a slew of problems and generate several successes. The return on investment for the latter would be significant, a concept that was pure gold and one we employed throughout our subsequent innovation journey at Edwards, sending members of our workforce for educational opportunities at places like Disney, Stanford, MIT, and USC. This also created a powerful incentive for those who were considering full-scale participation on our innovation team. By participating, they could receive valuable educational opportunities while rubbing shoulders with senior leaders.

Chief Eishen passed the job interview with flying colors, making my decision an easy one. When the time came to fill the Senior Enlisted Leader position, I hired him as the next Command Chief of The Center of the Aerospace Testing Universe. Thus, our trip to Beale was a success on multiple levels.

Around this time, we had an emergent, real-world test, requiring us to break barriers to meet immediate combat needs. It was a chance for our burgeoning innovative culture to prove itself with the world watching and the warfighter waiting.

The F-35 program office had become aware of a problem with its Navy and Marine Corps F-35s that limited their ability to fully employ and train at night. The operational community had determined that the existing F-35 air refueling probe light was inadequate for KC-135 drogue operations, and an immediate fix was needed. Word of this quickly made its way to Edwards, and the team sprang into action, punctuating the meaning of national strategy that called for "delivering performance at the speed of relevance."

The workforce at Edwards was not sitting idly by waiting for this urgent need. In fact, the F-35 test team was busy testing new combat software, qualifying the automatic ground collision avoidance system, and certifying F-35s to refuel behind the KC-46. Tanker test professionals were also busy certifying F-35 and C-130 receivers paired with the KC-46 and preparing for certification of B-2 and F-22 receivers. They were also engaged in writing numerous reports to support the KC-46 fielding decision. Additionally, tanker test teams were busy testing fixes to KC-135 autopilot software to incorporate into future operational software. The entire team was already focused on important warfighter needs, but this particular requirement was too important to let linger. Thus, the unleashed Edwards team shuffled manpower and resources to plan, support, execute, and report on this F-35 test program with minimal interruption to their other important priorities.

The Navy and Marine Corps test team resident at Edwards crafted an initial test plan reviewed by the Air Force team charged with executing the testing. In less than a month, test professionals created integrated test and safety plans to ensure test adequacy and apply proper risk management while maintaining constant communication with the F-35 and tanker program offices. They then crafted an innovative concept for ground testing of lighting alternatives in a blacked-out hangar and selected the one most likely to resolve the concerns. To verify this fix, they completed flight testing in operationally relevant conditions. The success of the modified air refueling probe light was quickly delivered to the F-35 program office, driving an immediate fielding decision to lift nighttime restrictions.

This showcased the agility and innovative spirit of those charged with shaping and molding America's arsenal through developmental test and evaluation. It didn't require a declaration of test acceleration, the establishment of a Joint Urgent Operational Need, up-front funding from the program office, or a formal task passed down through the chain of command. It only needed the dedication of a test team determined to meet the needs of the warfighter by delivering performance at the speed of relevance. They broke down barriers as they sprinted to meet operational needs, embracing the unleashed mindset I had hoped for in our innovation journey.

Around that same time, we had convened a formal Sprint by following the guidance of a book by the same name. As the book's subtitle suggests, Sprints can allow organizations to "solve big problems and test new ideas in just five days." According to its author and Google alumnus, Jake Knapp, such a week-long process "worked for all kinds of customers, from investors to farmers, from oncologists to small-business owners. It worked for websites, iPhone apps, paper medical reports, and high-tech hardware. And it wasn't just for developing products. We've used sprints for prioritization, for marketing strategy, even for naming companies. Time and again, the process brings teams together and brings ideas to life." We needed to harness such a concept to resolve a chronic problem we were facing at Edwards.

FLASHBACK TO JOINT BASE ANDREWS (2017)

I had convened a Sprint once before at Andrews when our workforce grappled with a major burnout problem. Being at the highest-visibility military base on the planet while commuting daily on the D.C. Beltway will do that to you. Yet, we sensed that there were other root causes to the problem that we could tackle to mitigate those challenges.

> I asked an extremely capable mid-level officer named Major Katy "DIME" Tenpenny to lead the week-long Sprint. Hesitant to accept at first, her leadership of that remarkable Sprint team led to mind-blowing outcomes. As a result of their findings and solutions, we adjusted the entire wing and wing commander schedule to create a more sustainable and predictable pace for the entire workforce. These shifts made a sizable dent in burnout concerns across the base, giving DIME the confidence to go on to do amazing things during the rest of her Air Force career.

While the workload at The Center of the Aerospace Testing Universe was substantial, there was another prevailing problem that created a cross-cutting concern at Edwards. A large portion of the workforce was made up of government civilians. These professionals provided amazing continuity in mission accomplishment throughout the base, and any gaps in civilian positions would create substantial problems for our ability to achieve our important mission.

Despite this, several vacancies in our workforce remained unfilled due to the extremely slow civilian hiring process. As a result, we were effectively missing over ten percent of our personnel as civilian positions sat vacant. The hiring process, characterized by its unimpressive glacial speed, prompted the need for a Civilian Hiring Sprint. Jessi Benveniste, a mid-level government civilian and rising star in our engineering workforce, was the perfect leader for such an effort.

Jessi and her team got to work, and the senior leadership team received updates and opportunities for input at the appropriate times throughout the week. We began adjusting the portions of the civilian hiring process that we had control over at Edwards, while advocating for adjustments in the portions controlled by our higher headquarters that would result in a significant and positive trickle-down effect at our wing and others around our large command.

In between the processes controlled by Edwards and our higher headquarters rested an additional organization that needed to adjust their processes in order to provide oversized impact in solving our problems. So, it was time to make another trip, this time to Hill Air Force Base, Utah where these civilian hiring human resource experts were based. It was time to Charge the Hill!

In reality, the trip was a charm offensive rather than the aggressive and mean-spirited intent implied by its name. Our wing's senior civilian, Daniel "Dan-O" Osburn, and I traveled north to visit these geographically-separated professionals and explain our critical mission at Edwards and their important role in supporting us. We wanted to build bonds of trust and togetherness through an intentional investment of our time with them. The charm offensive worked, and they were blown away by our visit. Never in their history did they have a base leadership team come to visit them.

We started our schedule in Utah with a mission overview to help explain the massive role Edwards played in shaping and molding America's aerospace arsenal and how they played a major part in us doing so. We outlined our civilian hiring problem, including what we were doing about it and what we were asking from the higher headquarters. Finally, we shared some process improvement recommendations that they might consider to help with this collective effort. Our trip opened a dialogue and created relationships that yielded massive fruit in our civilian hiring efforts.

As a follow-on to our visit to Hill, we invited them to join us for a few days at Edwards, even offering to pay for their trip with our wing funds. This would allow them to experience our mission first-hand and spend time working alongside our human resource experts that they had otherwise never met in person. In a simple one-day visit, we had created a partnership that would be essential in breaking down the personnel barriers that were crippling our mission and hindering the well-being of our workforce.

The results of both the Sprint and visit to Hill were staggering. In a short period of time, we adjusted our processes at Edwards to resolve our internal issues. Some of the help we needed from higher headquarters was eventually approved at their level as well, becoming a template for command-wide improvements. The biggest adjustments came from our engagement with the team from Hill as they became adopted members of our team and grew into passionate advocates for making improvements to help our mission.

The trip to Hill was nothing like the winter in Valley Forge for the Continental Army, but the intentional time we invested to build bonds and create community enabled its success. Our paralyzing civilian vacancies plummeted, so much so that it created a short-term civilian pay problem that had been masked by the hiring delays. The Sprint was a success, capped off by the oversized effectiveness of a face-to-face engagement by two leaders who Charged the Hill!

ACTION ITEMS

Action Item 1: Seek opportunities to connect with those you can learn from in your innovation journey and take time to see their operation in person.

Action Item 2: Use innovation resources to educate the members of the workforce who will become your innovation leaders.

Action Item 3: Consider a Sprint to solve a particularly challenging situation in your organization.

Action Item 4: Visit key stakeholders that are affiliated with your organization and help tie them into your mission. They will become passionate advocates for you if you do.

CHAPTER SEVEN

DAD JOKES

As World War II was coming to a close in Europe in the spring of 1945, British leaders mobilized in order to acquire notable German aviation technology for subsequent Allied use and prevent the Russians from doing the same. British Royal Navy test pilot Lieutenant Eric "Winkle" Brown was named the commanding officer of the Enemy Aircraft Flight and tasked with leading the British contingent on their mission into Germany. Lieutenant Brown's team entered the rubble of post-war Germany in the spring of 1945 to collect the Luftwaffe's best technology as Allied ground forces gained German territory.

Lieutenant Brown's initial experiences as the war was ending were extremely unique in a chaotic environment. During this period, he and his team flew to Denmark to exploit Germany's jet reconnaissance bomber, the Arado 234B. Using Army intelligence, he expected Allied occupation of Grove Airfield where the Arados were based. Unbeknownst to him, the Allies were slow in their advance, and his landing at Grove was, instead, at an active German airfield.

Fortunately, the German commanding officer surrendered upon arrival, and Lieutenant Brown controlled the airfield and its 2,000 men until Allied ground troops arrived the next day. Such a challenging environment demanded a leader with the right type of risk tolerance, even if it was occasionally miscalculated like his early arrival at Grove.

As we approached the kickoff for our innovation campaign at the end of the 116-Day Innovation Blitz, the Senior Innovation Council and Hustle Squad were fully engaged in preparation activities. Based on the feedback received on the Blitz, we expected to be bombarded with an arsenal of ideas, which would require us to be properly calibrated to *listen, consider,* and *act*.

During our preparation activities, we realized that Edwards did not have the indigenous expertise to properly pursue our innovation journey. With a slew of major components necessary to successfully pull off such a campaign, we wanted to remove any barriers or hindrances that would stand in our way. We realized the need for practical assistance in managing such a campaign, capturing the attention of our workforce, standing out above the ambient noise of base-wide activity, and fully conceptualizing innovation and organizational transformation.

This conclusion resonated well with a key component of my leadership philosophy—leaders must be characterized by a combination of humility and wisdom, a concept that almost escaped me when I nearly launched the innovation campaign without discussing it with my Senior Leadership Council. Even though the buck stops at the top of the chain of command, leaders are not expected to make unilateral decisions unsupported by the wealth of available expertise and resources. Leaders often get themselves in trouble when they try to tackle their job with the bravado of a solo leadership master.

Leadership wisdom includes the span of available resources and tools as a part of the decision-making process. Leadership humility is stepping down from the ivory tower of authority and reaching out to experts to *listen, consider,* and *act*. In this way, the concepts of leadership humility and wisdom are very much aligned with the definition of innovation guiding our journey at Edwards.

CHAPTER SEVEN ♠ **DAD JOKES** | 63

As I mentor subordinate leaders on this topic, I typically provide an example from my early leadership experience. In the Air Force, first-time commanders go through a week-long course to arm them with leadership tools that will help start off their position in the best possible way. One of the focuses is a presentation by an experienced legal team on military justice. At the end of their briefing during my course, these experts left a massive volume entitled *The Military Commander and the Law* with the commanders-to-be. I did a quick scan through it and realized it was filled with detailed legal arguments and jargon that made my eyes quickly glaze over. It was a thorough and well-researched resource, but I committed to never opening it again, and I encourage the same from others. Here's why.

If I have a thorny military legal issue, why should I think that I can make myself more of an expert than the resident military legal team at my base? They are the experts, and, instead of consulting a textbook, I should consult them. The final decision is ultimately up to me as the leader, and I would never blindly follow the advice of my experts, but basic knowledge in a subject is very different from studying it with focus.

In this example, I should ask the legal team thorough and tough questions to ensure I receive the complete picture of the legal issues and full range of decisions. During that discussion, we should also thoroughly address the costs, benefits, and risks of each decision. Additionally, a challenging issue does not typically stay in one lane of expertise, and my wisdom and humility should prompt me to talk to other experts in tangentially related areas to consider the secondary and tertiary impacts of a decision. The more consequential the decision, the more diligent I should be in my dedication to the leadership concepts of wisdom and humility.

> Matt Emmons was an accomplished competitive marksman. At the 2004 Summer Olympic Games in Athens, Greece, he had already won a gold medal and was on the verge of an unprecedented second. Through 129 shots in the competition, he held a commanding lead and only needed a marginal score on his final shot to secure the victory. On his last 50-meter shot, his precise shooting allowed

him to nail the target…on the wrong lane, an error so costly that, instead of finishing first, he finished eighth. In doing so, he provided an important reminder to all leaders—as sure as we may be that we are aiming at the right target, a healthy dose of humility and wisdom may give us the information we need to adjust our aim before it is too late.

The critical concepts of wisdom and humility should span every leader's decision-making portfolio, regardless of position. Leaders do not have all the answers, and will make much better decisions if they acknowledge this fact and create an environment where members of the team can raise concerns before they turn into problems. Openness and a free flow of information will allow a leader to make the best decisions possible while avoiding major missteps of unforeseen consequences. After all, hitting the wrong target can be disastrous for you and your organization. Additionally, completely harnessing the power of expertise and maximizing the utilization of your resources will magnify your impact and influence, pave the way for success, and boost the unity within your team. These factors were exactly what we needed to smoothly chart the course on our bold innovation journey.

FLASHBACK TO JOINT BASE ANDREWS (2017)

For the Air Force's 70th birthday celebratory activities we were tasked with at Joint Base Andrews, a three-day airshow was planned, a magnificent event that had been absent on the base-wide calendar for a decade. This event had traditionally been performed in the springtime, but, in order to align it with the celebration, it was shifted to the fall. Major Will Sack was our airshow lead, responsible for an activity that would be the capstone of the Air Force wide celebration. As we approached the date of the event, he had a major concern about the availability of ample parking for the expected crowd.

When he first approached me, I listened to his concern but didn't understand it because we had easily managed the need for parking space in the past, utilizing nearby FedEx Field and employing the use of rented buses to shuttle the crowds to and from base. However, he reminded me that the event, now being held in the fall, coincided with football season. Should the (then) Washington Redskins have a home game, their parking lots would be unavailable for use. With the dots now connected, I asked him for his recommended solution.

Major Sack filled me in on the available, alternative parking options, but none of them would be adequate to meet our requirements. He pitched one final option—to reach out to the NFL commissioner and ask him to schedule the (then) Redskins for an away game on that day. It was a non-traditional but brilliant suggestion!

To vet this idea, I reached out to my contact at the (then) Washington Redskins to make sure they didn't object to our plan. Our amazing community partners had already smoothed the way to secure their support. With their blessing, I signed a letter from me to Roger Goodell that Major Sack drafted, and Chief Perry dropped it in the mail.

Within two weeks, I received an official NFL envelope containing a letter with the Lombardi trophy embossed on the top of the stationary directly from Roger Goodell. He expressed his appreciation for those who serve our country in uniform and assured me that, after consulting with his experts and confirming with the (then) Redskins, Washington would not have a home game on that Sunday in September. When the schedule came out shortly thereafter, Washington was slated to play in Los Angeles on that day —as far away from D.C. as possible.

I am thankful that Major Will Sack had the wisdom to recognize the parking concern and the courage to raise the issue to me while there was still time to address it. He also offered a creative, viable solution that worked, and that was made possible by the backing of our remarkable community partners. Equally important was enough of a proper dose of leadership wisdom and humility to listen to him. If either of us had handled this differently, there would have been a 50/50 chance that our three-day airshow would have been truncated to a two-day event. And though our shot would have been precise, we would have struck the wrong target and our airshow would have suffered as a result.

Marching down the path of our innovation journey at Edwards, we needed our own dose of wisdom and humility. We had volunteered to be the Air Force-wide guinea pigs for the demonstration of innovative transformation at scale. We were a natural fit because of our culture of test and evaluation and our willingness to tackle the hard challenges that had faced the Air Force since its founding in 1947. At our core, we were scientists who formed, tested, and validated hypotheses in the world of cutting-edge aerospace. While there was risk that came from being an innovation pathfinder, there were some unique resources associated with it as well.

Air Force Secretary Heather Wilson announced the launch of AFWERX in July of 2017 with a charge to be "the innovation arm of the Department of the Air Force." They had a hub in Las Vegas, a mere three hours from our location at The Center of the Aerospace Testing Universe. It was an easy drive to get there, with the world's tallest thermometer in Baker, California marking the halfway point.

AFWERX had established an ecosystem of innovation talent that included a connection to classes and seminars providing a springboard for those promoting and fostering cultural transformation. Our Hustle Squad and Senior Innovation Council took full advantage of those resources in addition to grabbing on to other key offerings that accompanied our first-mover status.

AFWERX purchased a license to run innovation campaigns on IdeaScale, an innovation management platform created by a software company with the same name. That product provided the structure upon which to build our crowd-sourced idea collection and development campaign, removing the need to create such a complicated thing ourselves.

AFWERX had also contracted with The Difference and Gapingvoid Culture Design Group, two consulting firms that would help us with the practical and conceptual components of our innovation campaign in ways that we could never achieve with our indigenous expertise.

While we would eventually need to fund the contracts with these experts from our own traditional budget, we were able to start our efforts with a boost from AFWERX and their contracts that had been established with the hope of finding a base-level organization to fully employ them. And that we did!

Jason Korman, the CEO of Gapingvoid Culture Design Group, is a shaggy-haired professorial figure from Miami, Florida. He is not the kind of person you typically rub shoulders with in the military, and, after working with a variety of contractors in different venues throughout my career, I found that he was unlike anyone from my other experiences. Not only was he an innovation guru (seemingly literally), but he embodied a contagious passion for cultural transformation.

I particularly liked the fact that he reached out to me, personally, as the organization's leader in order to coach me and shape my thinking about our campaign and journey. Our conversations were always perspective-building and eye-opening. My team regularly received this type of graduate-level innovation education in the lead up to our campaign launch. Some of the consultant recommendations were non-traditional and required a leadership leap-of-faith from the commander.

The Hustle Squad and Senior Innovation Council worked full-time preparing for our campaign, collaborating daily with AFWERX and our contractor support team. They were excited about the prospects for success but recognized the risk that came with some of the methods we would use to communicate with the workforce. Despite having gotten to know me a bit, they were not entirely comfortable with requesting my full stamp of approval and participation as a part of their plans. Fortunately for all of us, it was around that time that I held a base-wide Commander's Call.

Commander's Calls are typically a quarterly way for commanders to meet with their team and provide the opportunity for a leader to speak directly to their entire organization. In our case at Edwards, we consumed the entire base theater, with livestream and recorded versions being available for those who could not fit into the facility or whose shift schedules would not allow them to join us in person. I loved these venues because they provided me with a chance to connect with the entire team at once and communicate in a way that was intended to be inspiring, encouraging and educating. My Command Chief and I would each cover important topics then hand out quarterly awards to our star performers. At the end, we would field questions from the audience.

If you have ever been a part of a massive meeting, you may have noticed that soliciting questions from a huge audience usually produces a prolonged and awkward silence. Few people are willing to speak in such a venue when the forum does not allow for a fun and informative communication pathway or spark a free flow of questions and answers.

FLASHBACK TO JOINT BASE ANDREWS (2016-2018) & EDWARDS AFB (2008)

While at Andrews, a colleague suggested using anonymous texting to break this predictable logjam, a simple solution that worked. For our Q&A session, we would display our Command Chief's cell phone number, and he would read off questions as they came in. We encouraged the audience to be creative and enjoy themselves, asking for a mix of funny and serious questions to intersperse into the pacing of our responses.

We often got questions about a big upcoming sport event—"Are you rooting for the Cowboys or the Patriots?"—or questions about culture and society—"Do you like DC or Marvel comics?" We also got inquiries about the base—"Why are we not replacing the bowling alley that was damaged beyond repair by the most recent earthquake?" and provocative questions about the workplace—"When will we prioritize replacing the headquarters and laboratory facility for engineers?" During almost every Commander's Call, someone would ask me for my latest favorite "dad joke."

My dad joke journey started when I was "forced" to wear an elf costume to our unit's Christmas and Holiday Party after receiving the most votes to do so in order to raise money for the squadron morale fund. I figured that, if I had to wear a costume like that at such an event, I would make the audience endure a slew of elf jokes throughout night. I memorized about three dozen and would grab the microphone every few minutes to tell one as I performed a little elf dance, intentionally being playful and obnoxious. My material received a lot of groans, but I realized that it also provided a disarming way to break down barriers with a variety of people, so I've employed that method ever since.

Needless to say, the anonymous text idea worked, and similarly to Dragon's Lair, the floodgates opened. We typically didn't have time to answer all the questions at the event, but we covered as many as we could! When our scheduled time ended, we stopped the Commander's Call but answered the remaining questions as Dragon's Lair inputs on the app for all to see, leaving no hanging chads.

Around the time the Hustle Squad was sizing me up for the big reveal about the details of our upcoming innovation campaign, we had our quarterly Commander's Call. The questions did not disappoint, and as is typically the case, they asked me for a "dad joke." My favorite (which I'm not going to share here) is one whose punchline requires singing. I am a horrible singer. Yet, when I tell the punchline, I pour my full energy into the performance. The delivery prompts a good laugh, though I'm not quite sure whether it is at or with me, but it doesn't really matter.

At this Commander's Call, I felt compelled to tell that joke. It went off well, especially due to my brilliant falsetto ending. Most importantly, it convinced Chris Klug and the others on our Senior Innovation Council that I was radical enough for the non-traditional elements of our innovation campaign. The joke broke the last bit of ice between me and our team (and would have probably shattered a crystal glass if one were around). Though my situation was a bit different from the wartime experience of Lieutenant Eric "Winkle" Brown, my risk tolerance was proven to be properly calibrated to the needs of our upcoming innovation journey. It was time to start the campaign!

ACTION ITEMS

Action Item 1: Enlist outside help to support the goals of your innovation journey.

Action Item 2: Infuse your leadership persona with a healthy dose of humility and wisdom.

Action Item 3: Deliberately create conditions that allow yourself to be accessible and even vulnerable.

CHAPTER EIGHT

AN INNOVATION MANIFESTO

Jimmy Doolittle, Eddie Rickenbacker, and Charles Lindbergh were early American aviation heroes. They were world-renowned aviators, each receiving the Congressional Medal of Honor during their lifetimes. Doolittle was an inter-war test pilot and speedster who held several world records and proved the viability of instrument guided flight. Rickenbacker, a race car driver turned pilot, had racked up America's most air-to-air kills during World War I. Lindbergh was an air mail pilot who gained worldwide fame for his record-breaking transatlantic flight. They were all iconic. Interestingly, though, they each had the same strange individual experience in Germany in the late 1930s that telegraphed the impending challenges that the world would face from a resurgent Germany military power.

Ernest Udet was a German World War I flying ace and the architect of the powerful inner-war German Air Force known as the Luftwaffe. Knowing the aviation credibility of Doolittle, Rickenbacker, and Lindberg, Udet separately invited them for a visit to witness the amazing German aviation capabilities while sharing detailed stories of plans to reestablish the German Empire through the air. Udet even engaged these American heroes in shooting competitions in his audacious and oddly decorated apartment.

It was as if Udet, on behalf of the German leaders, was flaunting their military buildup and militant prowess as America sat passively on the sidelines with an isolationist fervor that swept across our nation following the demobilization after World War I. Though these three American icons spoke out about their observations to senior American leaders upon their return, it was not enough to shake the country out of its complacency.

The keystone to the launch of our innovation campaign at Edwards was a video that described our transformational vision and mission. Yet, it did not do so in the traditional bureaucratic way characterized by productions that have too many words with too little meaning. It was provocative and captivating, designed to shake our Edwards workforce out of its complacency. We created a three and half minute video entitled the *Innovation Manifesto*.

We carefully crafted the words of this manifesto to capture the attention of our workforce, hoping they would be unsettled and shocked by it. We aimed to ignite conversations, challenge assumptions, and tie our entire workforce together. We wanted the broader team to see something different than anything they expected to be sanctioned by a senior leader. It was not gratuitous or graphic, but it was thought-provoking and compelling. It broke the mold of the tired and traditional, forcing everyone who watched it to think and consider the complacent and defiant pathway we were collectively on if we didn't take drastic steps to make massive changes to our organizational culture!

We filmed from a location that overlooked the main portion of the base. We wanted it to be an overarching charge for our 304,000-acre installation and everyone who drove through our gates. I played what seemed like the primary role in the video, saying things that still provoke me today. We designed the content to be as bold as we wanted our workforce to be in their pursuit of our cultural transformation. The following lines are some of my favorites from the final video:

- "The conflict will be won by the best minds, not by the most might."

CHAPTER EIGHT ♠ AN INNOVATION MANIFESTO | 73

- "We aid our adversaries every time we fail to get to YES."
- "We must welcome a mindset to do things differently; we must embrace fearlessness in everything we do."
- "Tired traditional thinking will ensure we lose the next conflict."
- "We will lose and we will suffer if our cowardice today causes us to avoid the risk of doing things differently."
- "This is a call to arms for all of us who care, who want to make a difference, and who cherish our freedom."
- "We need your commitment to act with courage and boldness; our nation needs us to make history today."
- "Join us today!"

It was also vital that the video feature more than just me. Regularly interspersed throughout the manifesto were clips and quotes from the Hustle Squad. After all, this was their movement, and to some extent, I was just a prop. They were the real main actors. My words throughout the video are simply an amplification of their provocative prompts. Many of the most captivating quotes came from them, still resonating powerfully with me and with all who watch it:

- "Our adversaries want to harm and destroy us."
- "We are at risk and must take bold action."
- "It is an uncomfortable journey, but one we must accept."
- "We must not hide behind rules and regulations."
- "We have proudly started an innovation movement."
- "We say NO to those who cling to the past."
- "Join us! Join us! Join us! Join us! Join us!"

Their words were directed precisely to the heart and soul of our workforce, like a laser-guided missile. When our broader team watched the video, they saw these members of the force who were truly leading the movement, providing powerful, visual confirmation of their leader's support. It was not a movement facilitated by top-down direction, rather a protected, bottom-up eruption of directed passion and energy that had been brewing as an untapped resource for many years.

We were not going to simply send out the *Innovation Manifesto* without fanfare. Instead, we scheduled pep rallies at key locations around the base to roll-out the video with gusto and speak directly to the force. It was the day of our innovation launch, and this was the main event for the base. And while I played a major role in the pep rally delivery, I was always flanked by Hustle Squad members who provided direction to the assembled crowds about how to participate in a movement they were officially unleashing on that day.

One of the best lines used during the base-wide pep rallies came from Robert Louis Stevenson who wrote, "So soon as prudence has begun to grow up in the brain, like a dismal fungus, it finds its first expression in a paralysis of generous acts." These words provided a powerful pictorial of our intent. The seemingly prudent adherence to the status quo actually choked out progress. It caused a rot within our organizational soul and paralyzed the positive motion we needed to achieve our mission and improve our quality of life. This campaign was designed to shine a bright spotlight into the dark and dreary areas of organizational culture that existed at Edwards while prompting a superbloom of life-yielding ideas.

The video was a hit, and the energy provided by the Hustle Squad was contagious. The workforce saw the activities not as a grandstanding senior leader but as an exciting change that started at the lowest level of the hierarchical pyramid. The innovation team liberally handed out swag with our campaign theme and logo emblazoned across—t-shirts, posters, stickers, pamphlets and pens that stood out in their unique designs and atypical slogans. They also directed the workforce to the online tools used to operationalize the campaign. In an instant, these items made their way to every corner of the organization, and along with the pep rallies, they created a buzz that we expected to add fuel to feed the thrust of cultural transformation we so desperately needed at The Center of the Aerospace Testing Universe. We were igniting a social contagion that would break through the classic barriers to innovation.

The Innovation Manifesto, in video form, was as a great way to reach people, but we wanted to package it in a more personalized fashion. So, we created a manifesto book and held an old-fashioned base-wide book signing. The lines for signature were out the door for the event, and it gave people a chance to pick up and display a keepsake of the innovation movement sweeping the base. Having a book in one's possession indicated that its owner was a part of the movement and committed to its success. Additionally, we distributed unsigned books throughout the base, and even until the last day of my tenure as the Edwards commander, people would track me down for a signature. This journey became more than a tasker, directive, or campaign—it was a full-blown movement!

A few days after the pep rally launch of our innovation journey, I found myself serendipitously standing with Heidi in the company of the Vice Chief of Staff, General Stephen Wilson, and the Director of Staff of the Air Force, Lieutenant General Jacqueline Van Ovost. They held the number two and three positions in the service's hierarchy. We had a chance to show them the *Innovation Manifesto* video, and as it played, we watched their faces. We didn't know how they would react, but they were positively and successfully provoked.

Heidi had the opportunity to brief these two leaders on our innovation movement, and she killed it! There was no coordination or preparation between the two of us about what she was going to say. Frankly, the engagement was largely an ad hoc opportunity that only materialized at the last minute at the AFWERX facility in Las Vegas. I trusted Heidi, and she earned every bit of that trust. Her words and her passion impressed those senior leaders so much that General Wilson gave her a highly coveted Commander's coin on the spot. Heidi claims that she mentally blacked out after that experience, and when she heard a recording of his voice several years later, it caused her to break down in tears of overwhelming joy at the magnitude of the moment.

Word spread beyond Edwards that, when you were on the Hustle Squad or a major part of the innovation movement, it gave you opportunities that would be otherwise absent in one's career. Heidi still considers that engagement as one of the high points of her lifetime and used that experience to fuel her leadership of the Hustle Squad going forward.

These two leaders asked what they could do to support Edwards as we paved the way for transformation and innovation at scale for the rest of the Air Force. I had a bold response on the ready—I asked them to delegate all waiver authority from the headquarters of the Air Force to me for activities at Edwards Air Force Base! After all, the United States Air Force already trusts their wing commanders with a lot of authority and responsibility. In my case in test and evaluation, I was the approval authority for high-risk test missions with priceless test assets. If the Air Force institution could trust me with that type of decision-making authority, then it should be able to trust me with decision-making authority to waive various administrative rules and regulations. If I got the former wrong, it had far greater consequences than the latter.

The leaders paused and described a very attractive alternative to my request. There was a little-known loophole in the regulation-on-regulations that allowed far greater waiver authority at the commander level than anybody realized. Lieutenant General Van Ovost shared that secret with me and recommended that I use it to its fullest extent. She also promised that if I found that authority to be insufficient, they would consider providing me the broader waiver authority I had originally asked for. Frankly, I was disappointed that I hadn't fully understood the extent of my authority but was excited to exploit this loophole.

All of the innovation campaign activities up to this point were meant to create a buzz with the explicit intent of convincing our workforce to join our movement. We didn't want it to be a leader convincing them, rather an environment that prompted them to convince themselves. In their minds, it needed to be a journey that was legitimate, desperately needed, in their best interest, and to be trusted. After all, we wanted their ideas, but first we needed them to commit to our journey together. We also wanted to saturate their environment such that they could not miss our full-fledged commitment to *listening, considering,* and *acting.*

CHAPTER EIGHT ♣ AN INNOVATION MANIFESTO | 77

Every member of our force was bombarded with reminders of our campaign. They would arrive at work and park next to cars with bumper stickers about it. They would walk in from the parking lot and be greeted with campaign chalk art on the sidewalks. They would enter their workplaces and be met with images of it. They would walk down the halls to their offices and see campaign posters. They would sit down at their desks littered with campaign swag pens and pamphlets and the manifesto book. They would turn on their computer and see our campaign video. We sent targeted emails from the Hustle Squad about it. The on-base restaurants had campaign placemats and napkins. Members of the workforce would go home at the end of the day, and their spouses would mention the family version of our campaign and their kids would mention the student version of it. It was what the experts call relentless socialization.

This wasn't a flashy, short-term phenomenon. It continued throughout the 70-day campaign and beyond, making it clear to the population that it wasn't a fad event or flash in the pan. It was becoming who we were and what we wanted to be known for. The logos and images were designed to be different, unlike anything else the workforce had seen on bumpers, sidewalks, office walls, office desks, emails, or restaurant tables. They were designed to contrast with the uninspired standard to avoid being filtered out by the pattern-matching portion of the human mind. They would lead to important conversations and telegraph the intent and willingness of the leadership team to take risks and do things differently.

Our partners at Gapingvoid worked with the Hustle Squad to create the material that stood out from the norm and resonated in a targeted way with our workforce. One of the of the most gripping visual artifacts of the campaign was the creation of Culture Walls, a series of 12 by 12-inch tiles containing unique images and provocative statements that sprung up in the entryways of offices around the base. The Hustle Squad worked with individual organizations at Edwards to design the walls in a way that would be particularly powerful for their unit, mission and people. We unveiled our wing-wide Culture Wall in the headquarters as a part of the pep rally and hinged our subsequent talking points on many of the slogans inscribed on the 20 individual tiles that hung on the wall for all to see. They included the following:

- "Stagnation equals death."
- "If it isn't a law, then it's just a suggestion."
- "Innovation, it shouldn't take a war."

My favorite slogan was "Find out where 'no' lives and kill it!" If you haven't figured it out by now, I really don't like the amount of "No" responses that stand in the way of progress. The Culture Wall tile with this slogan still proudly hangs in my office. I've carried it with me to a 14-month deployment in Baghdad, Iraq and to my assignment in the Pentagon. It is now prominently displayed in my home office, and it brings a smile to my face as I look at it as I type these words. I would hang it in the Oval Office if I were President.

The experts use a fancy term for the power of statements and images that effectively capture the attention of human beings—memetics. As a gene is a building block of life, a meme is a building block of culture. Similarly, as genetics pass on human characteristics, memetics pass on cultural characteristics. As genetics form the basis for individual life, memetics form the basis for organizational life. Memetics, like genetics, are catchy, sticky, and powerful. They transmit their messages effectively despite looming barriers and can have widespread, multi-generational impact. Yet, there is another concept at play in issues of organizational culture that makes the power of memetics an important tool in counteracting the alluring trappings of the status quo.

Thomas Kuhn wrote *The Structure of Scientific Revolutions* in 1962. As a PhD physicist from Harvard, his post-doctoral studies led him to an interest in the history and philosophy of science and human cognition. His work popularized the phrases "paradigm" and "paradigm shift" by describing the extreme power of the mental frameworks that embody a paradigm. A paradigm fundamentally shapes our ability to see our environment. "What a man sees depends both upon what he looks at and also upon what his previous visual-conceptual experience has taught him to see."

CHAPTER EIGHT ♣ AN INNOVATION MANIFESTO | 79

A paradigm prevents dissent. "Subsequent practice will seldom evoke overt disagreement over fundamentals." And, most pessimistically, Kuhn claims that paradigms can only be shifted by a crisis. "Crises are a necessary precondition for the emergence of novel theories." Paradigms have prompted failures in scientific understanding, major political missteps, and even deadly airplane crashes, including a tragedy that I endured previously at Edwards when we lost an F-22 and a mentor, friend, and hero, David "Cools" Cooley. It was a gut-wrenching experience, one that I have shared as a preventative measure with thousands of people around the country. Most recently, I shared it with Congressional staffers in the U.S. Capitol.

While most agree with Kuhn about the power of paradigms, there are many who are less pessimistic about the human ability to design conditions to challenge and change paradigms. Those experts turn to various forms of provocative communication, like memetics, to change the paradigm without the painful process that would accompany a crisis. There is more scientific theory that describes organizational transformation than these important concepts, but these two ideas of memetics and paradigms were so fundamental to our innovation journey at Edwards, that a short detour into theory was necessary. Hopefully, these concepts spur some thought in your mind about the current paradigms of your organization and the necessary communication tools you must employ to preempt a looming crisis you may have not even considered.

The Innovation Manifesto, pep rallies, book signing, Culture Walls, and swag were all the right way to launch a campaign and give it the necessary thrust to succeed in shaking our workforce out of their complacency in a way that Doolittle, Rickenbacker, and Lindberg could not do with the U.S. Government after their meetings with Ernst Udet. Was it showmanship? Yes! Was it bravado? Yes! Was it relentless promotion? Yes! Was it bold and a bit risky? Heck yes! Yet, it was never self-aggrandizing or unauthentically ostentatious. It was all created for the furtherance of our mission and the betterment of our organization. We had cast a bold and captivating vision, diligently grabbing the spotlight of attention while promising to *listen* and *consider*. We were ready to *act* with determined follow-through. Most importantly, our innovation journey was structured with the Hustle Squad front and center as the embodiment of our innovation journey and the manifestation of our manifesto.

ACTION ITEMS

Action Item 1: Ignite transformation campaigns through saturation of the environment and relentless socialization of ideas, norms, concepts, values, and artifacts.

Action Item 2: Fully understand and wisely use the full extent of your leadership authority.

Action Item 3: Consider and employ the powerful concepts of paradigms and memetics.

Action Item 4: Lead with a bold and captivating vision, diligently grab the spotlight of organizational attention and maintain thorough and determined follow-through.

CHAPTER NINE

#INNOVATIVEAF

(AF MEANS AIR FORCE)

In the lead up to World War II, President Franklin Delano Roosevelt established the Office of Strategic Services (OSS), the precursor to today's Central Intelligence Agency (CIA). The OSS was responsible for coordinating and conducting intelligence-gathering, propaganda, and subversion activities for the United States. It was a carefully created organization based on the successful and highly regarded British MI-6.

In order to inform and guide the subversive activities of friendly workers behind enemy lines, the OSS published the *Simple Sabotage Field Manual* in January 1944. It was specifically written to support those individuals in occupied Europe to enable them to hinder the Axis war effort there and diminish the effectiveness of Germany's industrial wartime production.

In the manual's introduction, the OSS makes it clear that even those who are untrained can help with such efforts, saying, "Simple sabotage does not require specially prepared tools of equipment; it is executed by an ordinary citizen who may or may not act individually and without the necessity for active connection with an organized group; and it is carried out in such a way as to involve a minimum danger of injury, detection, and reprisal."

The OSS instructions are broken down into subversive activities that can be undertaken at the personal level and those that can be employed at the organizational level. At the personal level, the OSS's recommendations include the following:

- "A non-cooperative attitude may involve nothing more than creating an unpleasant situation among one's fellow workers, engaging in bickering, or displaying surliness and stupidity."
- "Give lengthy and incomprehensible explanations when questioned."
- "Act stupid"
- "Bring up irrelevant issues as frequently as possible."
- "Make speeches. Talk as frequently as possible and at great length. Illustrate your points by long anecdotes and accounts of personal experiences."

As you read through these, you are probably thinking about a handful of coworkers whose characteristics match these so perfectly that you are now wondering if they have been specifically employed by a hostile foreign power to subvert the effectiveness of your organization and paralyze the operations of your workforce. While it isn't impossible that the coworkers who popped into your mind are highly trained operatives, they may simply be naturally gifted at being subversive.

At the organizational level, the OSS recommends the following effective activities to subvert organizational effectiveness:

- "Insist on doing everything through channels."
- "Never permit short-cuts to be taken in order to expedite decisions."

- "When possible, refer all matters to committees, for further study and consideration."

- "Advocate caution."

- "Multiply paperwork in plausible ways."

- "Multiply the procedures and clearances involved in issuing instructions, pay checks, and so on."

- "See that three people have to approve everything where one would do."

Characteristics of organizational subversion are stunning to consider in light of our prevailing workplace structures and processes. In many cases, it seems as if our bureaucratic organizations are intentionally designed to hinder and subvert progress. *Doing everything through channels* is a precise summary of the painstaking pathways described by the extensive rules and regulations that govern our organizations. *Short cuts to expedite decisions* are reserved for special circumstances, considered fraught with risk, and to be avoided at all costs. *Committees and further studies* are the graveyards of new ideas and novel concepts. *Advocating caution* is bureaucratic code for a leader's lack of moral courage to deviate from the norm. *Multiplying paperwork, procedures, and clearances* are plausible and expected outcomes in our organizations because they are a natural part of our cherished processes. Finally, *three people where one would do* seems to be the standard within our hierarchical workplaces. It is actually the antithesis of trust that resists the proper delegation of authority to the right level in an organization.

We have all grown accustomed to multi-layer approval processes that cost valuable time and painfully indicate a lack of organizational trust. These long and drawn-out approval chains unnecessarily distribute risk, diffusing authority and responsibility. While such a process subverts progress, it also sabotages leadership authority by squashing considerations before a leader even has the opportunity to hear and consider them.

These approval mechanisms challenge any attempt to get to a final yes decision on a new idea, because a *no* decision at any step of the process will immediately kill an initiative and retain the status quo. Unanimity is the only pathway to approval, and a single dissent at any level will end debate and halt discussion without question. Some of the most powerful examples of this concept in my career occurred during my 14-month deployment to Baghdad, Iraq.

The simpler example ties into a comment I made in the previous chapter about the approval authority at Edwards for high-risk testing of a two-billion-dollar B-2 bomber. As the wing commander, I was the approval authority for such testing because it had been rightfully delegated to me by those above me in the chain of command. It was reasonable to maintain that decision-making authority at my level because it was a consequential decision spanning my scope of responsibility, but it was also one that was pushed down to my position because I was the most informed, highest-ranking leader with regular interaction about the particulars of the test as a natural part of my duties.

This sounds like a perfect formula for the delegation of authority: it should be pushed no lower than the position that can take responsibility for the full consequences of a decision but no higher than the position that is fully informed as a regular part of a leader's duties. In this case, decisions about high-risk testing were a perfect fit for the wing commander level, but other decision-making activities in my career have not been as well considered.

FLASHFORWARD TO IRAQ (2020-2021)

I was deployed to Iraq for 14-months during a particularly challenging time—May 2020 until July 2021. Iranian-aligned militia groups were acting on a regular basis to hinder the authority and sovereignty of the rightfully selected leaders of Iraq, and these Iranian-backed groups were still fuming about the American airstrike that had killed Iranian military leader Qasem Soleimani and the Iraqi militia leader Abu Mahdi al-Muhandis in early January 2020.

These groups expressed their displeasure through regular demands for a withdrawal of residual American forces in the country that were there at the invitation of the Iraqi government to support continued operations against the forces of the Islamic State (ISIS). These militia groups also expressed their anger by conducting regular rocket strikes on American personnel, including those at the U.S. Embassy in Baghdad, and by threatening to kidnap high ranking American military members. It was also a time during the heart of the COVID-19 pandemic where the public health risk calculus seemed to be changing every single day. Most of the planet was quarantined in their homes, but in our deployed environment, we had an important mission to accomplish. Thus, we worked together daily.

Rightfully, the U.S. Embassy in Baghdad had rules about security and public health that kept the population inside the embassy compound unless the mission required otherwise. During my time there, I traveled outside the embassy several times a week, typically for a weekly meeting with the Chief of Defense of the Iraqi military and periodic meetings with the Prime Minister's Personal Secretary or the leaders of the five military services in Iraq.

Those meetings were often within the protected International Zone (IZ—formerly named the Green Zone) but were sufficiently far enough away from the embassy that they required an escort by a comprehensive security detail. Additionally, because of COVID, there were the traditional limitations that required face masks and appropriate distancing, despite being a young and healthy population by the nature of our military and deployed status. The magnitude of such movements required Ambassador approval, which he had delegated to his deputy (the Deputy Chief of Mission or DCM for short). All of this was a proper example of sound decision-making pathways.

At the same time, Union 3, an allied military headquarters situated across the street from the embassy, was still within the protected IZ. My military team in the embassy had real mission needs that required regular trips back and forth between the two compounds. It was a short though slightly circuitous drive to transition between these adjoining locations. Residual security threats were reasonably mitigated by driving an armored vehicle with special training. Public health concerns were reasonably mitigated by normal COVID protocols for our healthy population.

However, it wasn't quite as simple as that in the minds of the senior diplomatic officials in the embassy. The Ambassador retained full decision-making authority to allow anyone to travel from one location to the other, only delegating that authority no further down than the DCM.

There were no supplemental security requirements needed for such a trip. All risks were understood and mitigated by our military organization. As the leader, I had full visibility into the mission needs requiring such a short trip and received daily updates on both the COVID status at each location and the security threats in the local environment. Yet, we had to ask permission to cross the street. That was a stunning contrast to a previous job where I was trusted to make decisions to perform high-risk testing on a B-2. It was an example of organizational sabotage that sapped initiative and bogged down progress. This, however, was not the worst example of mismatched decision-making levels.

The security situation grew tense for Americans in Iraq as we approached the 1 year anniversary of the killing of Soleimani and Muhandis. The State Department decided to evacuate the majority of the diplomatic personnel in Baghdad for a period that dragged on for nearly six months, and ninety percent of my organization was repositioned to Kuwait during that period. A few of us remained in Baghdad to continue performing the local mission the best we could and directly support the Ambassador.

During this time, the State Department closely controlled the numbers of American personnel in the embassy to abide by the constraints established by the Secretary of State and his senior leadership team. This was part of a reasonable decision-making process based on authority, responsibility, risk and visibility. Yet, they went overboard in their close control of our activities.

Instead of allowing the Ambassador to manage to the personnel constraints on his own within the limits of manpower caps, the State Department headquarters tightly controlled not only the numbers of personnel allowed in the Embassy but the individual names of the personnel in the Embassy. Any swaps of personnel required explicit approval by name from Washington, D.C., and it became a cumbersome, bureaucratic exercise to get approvals for simple manpower changes. Such a mismatch of decision-making authority consumed a large amount of the time and energy of the remaining, sparse personnel in Baghdad.

This situation revealed itself as completely broken when I took my first trip to visit my team that had been displaced to Kuwait. I purposefully didn't swap another member of our team from Kuwait into my slot in Baghdad so I would have the flexibility to return as needed without State Department approval. At least that was the flexibility I *thought* I was retaining by doing so. When it was time to return, I was told that the State Department needed to provide approval for such a swap. I argued that there was no swap needed, as my slot was vacant, but that wasn't the way the headquarters saw it. They proceeded to consume several man hours and a few extra days to get approval coordinated through 21 different people in State Department headquarters to swap Teichert for Teichert. I kept the extensively coordinated memorandum that authorized this movement because I could not believe it. It wasn't just three people where one would do; it was literally 21 people where even one was overkill. It was pure bureaucratic organizational sabotage.

This example was the diametric opposite of the playbook we were using in our innovation campaign at Edwards. In fact, it was the antithesis of our decision-making construct at The Center of The Aerospace Testing Universe during our cultural transformation.

The Hustle Squad had the lead for our innovation journey. While they would regularly keep me updated on their progress during our campaign, more for my situational awareness than for any other reason, there was no rationale for me to retain authority at my level.

The Senior Innovation Council was their daily interface, and together, they had the authorities, resources, and checks and balances to meet our bold vision. Other than major budgeting decisions or severe risk management situations, they were far more capable of making the day-to-day decisions that would guide our organizational transformation journey than I. They were free to allocate resources as they saw fit, even for the prioritization and optimization of ideas generated by the campaign, as long as they stayed within their budget.

I appreciated the occasional question from them about how I wanted to direct activities, and after a brief discussion that revealed my overall intent, my most frequent response became, "What do you recommend?" It was almost always the case that their recommendation became our direction. Frankly, good leaders who trust their teams should always ask such a question when an expert asks them for direction. A good team will have a reasonable answer, and while it may not be exactly what the leader would do, if it is reasonably safe and effective, then it is often the best path to take.

Falling back on the leadership construct from Chapter 5, I prioritized the following:

- Serving and supporting people and building relationships
- Casting a bold and compelling vision
- Setting broad limits in the pursuit of that vision
- Appropriately resourcing the achievement of that vision

- Breaking down barriers that hinder a workforce and block achievement of that vision

- Getting out of the way

Did the Hustle Squad need personal or personnel support? We would jump at the opportunity to provide it. Did they need a bold and compelling vision? Yes, and we had provided one in terms of our comprehensive definition of innovation—*listen, consider,* and *act*. Did they need broad limits in the pursuit of that vision? Maybe, but generally we trusted them to set those limits themselves and ask if they were concerned about exceeding a major parameter. Did they need resources? Yes, we provided those to them liberally. Did they need help breaking down barriers? Occasionally, and we jumped at the opportunity to do so. Did we get out of the way? Yes, because that was what unleashing our team was all about!

The initial innovation campaign was a huge success because of this mutually reinforcing cycle of trust, delegation of decision-making authority, saturation, socialization, and intentionally designed cultural change. As Figure 1.0 in the Introduction depicts, the team at The Center of the Aerospace Testing Universe dwarfed the innovation activity of the rest of the Air Force combined, based on ideas, engagement with ideas, and crowd-sourced selection of ideas. While these metrics are nice, a few stories will help reveal where organizational transformation was sprouting beyond a single campaign of ideas.

In the middle of 2019, Staff Sergeant Michael Meyer had a great idea —Edwards needed to host a TEDx event with a world-class lineup of speakers. He was a young F-22 maintainer, a budding innovator, and a member of our team with a good idea. As far as we knew, such an event would be one of the first in the Department of Defense and only the second in the United States Air Force. Such an event would create a buzz around base, further our ability to communicate to our workforce that they were a part of something special, create memories, and spark creativity that could be put to great use as we continued our innovation journey.

Sergeant Meyer and the Hustle Squad team asked me what I thought about having such an event. "What do you recommend?" I asked on cue. They quickly explained their recommendation and rationale. I said yes, and we set a date and location.

The timing would immediately precede our second major innovation campaign. The location would be in the world's biggest anechoic facility, conveniently located on Edwards. This massive testing asset is so big that even cargo planes can hang from the ceiling, and it is used so that no electromagnetic signals tested in the facility can leak out and nothing from the outside can leak in. Our hope, however, was that the surging innovation activity from the TEDx event would spread throughout and beyond the base. We used a prototype F-16XL as the backdrop for the stage and booked a world-class lineup. We had Kelly Latimer, veteran test pilot who had recently launched a rocket from a Boeing 747; Peter Newell, Silicon Valley innovation consultant and early-stage technology accelerator who broke down bureaucratic barriers for breakfast; Colonel Randel "Laz" Gordon who had recently stood up an artificial intelligence accelerator for the Air Force in collaboration with MIT and was a motivational and inspirational personality; and our own innovation juggernaut Chief Ian Eishen, to round out our slate of speakers. It was a remarkable event!

Most importantly, it was the brainchild of a young, enlisted member of our team. It was his concept, and he was responsible for leading its planning and execution. He did so brilliantly, and the event was a huge hit. The most important point here, however, is that this individual member of our team was able to express his voice. In a normal hierarchical organization, someone like Sergeant Meyer would be a cog in the wheel who was only expected to perform his daily maintenance tasks according to strict adherence to regulations—nothing more, nothing less. Yet, in this environment, he was able to create something magnificent.

Sergeant Meyer's idea became a memorable extravaganza that many would describe as the highlight of the year at a place known for its frequent ground-breaking highlights. In fact, it was such a hit that, after the COVID restrictions waned, the first large scale activity hosted by

Edwards was a second TEDx event to follow in the successful footsteps of the first. By now, they've probably hosted another one.

Down the flightline, other, more directly mission-related activity was occurring. The KC-46 Pegasus, the nation's next-generation air-to-air refueling aircraft, was completing its test and evaluation activities. There was a problem, however. A handful of major deficiencies with the system, especially related to the new remote vision system, arose to severely concerning levels. In such a situation, there are some perverse incentives for various government components to overlook such deficiencies to keep the delivery and fielding of such a large and expensive system on track and on schedule. Yet, it was the role of test and evaluation professionals to provide the unvarnished truth about the performance of the system, despite political forces that would apply maximum pressure to dampen such concerns.

The squadron commander of that test organization, Lieutenant Colonel Paul "PROMO" Calhoun, reached out to me to let me know that their assessment was leading them to formally and publicly submit a high-level deficiency report that reflected their concerns about the operational capability of the new tanker. PROMO was a humble servant leader and trusted expert who came from a prestigious DARPA fellowship and knew how to innovate and manage risk. He asked how I wanted to proceed, essentially asking whether I supported their submission of the deficiency, knowing that Edwards would face attacks for doing so. My question to PROMO was the same as always, "What do you recommend?" He recommended that we submit the deficiency. I followed up with another question, "In your expert opinion, does the deficiency report accurately characterize the system you and your team tested?" He replied with an emphatic, yes!

At that point, it was a no-brainer, and I told PROMO to submit it. My only request was that he educate me on the full extent of the concerns and keep me updated on all high-level deficiency report submissions in the future before they are filed, so I can prepare for the hate-mail I will ultimately receive from those who wanted their prized system to stay on track.

It takes a lot of courage for a squadron commander to put his reputation on the line in providing unpopular information. It would have a multi-billion-dollar ramification. Despite this, PROMO was willing to follow through because such integrity, professionalism, and courage were natural parts of who he was as a leader. It also reflected his trust in his own experts and my trust in him. That deficiency report is a natural extension of the listen, consider, and act cycle. The result of his courage and organization's expertise and zealous support of the warfighter was an extensive multi-year redesign of the deficient component of the system that is still occasionally grabbing headlines in the press today.

Trust requires courage, both up and down the chain. It is a lubricant of progress and catalyst of communication. Sometimes, it requires a leap of faith to create the habitual pattern of trust that will serve you and your organization well. Wilbur Wright said, "If you are looking for perfect safety, you will do well to sit on a fence and watch the birds; but if you really wish to learn, you must mount a machine and become acquainted with its tricks by actual trial."

None of this is to say that a leader should blindly trust in every circumstance. It becomes easier to trust if you have carefully hired the right people into the right positions on your team. It also becomes easier to trust when you have previously exercised it with positive outcomes, proving it to be legitimate and well-earned. It is best applied at first as a part of the less consequential decisions. Then it can mature into its application in the more consequential decisions.

Trust is solidified when it corresponds with a culture of honesty, integrity, and courage. The glue of trust is solidified when it enables your team to share both the good and bad news with a leader, and when members of the team self-identify when they make a mistake. Even with all of this in mind, the leader uses judgment and intuition about when to dig a bit deeper into the rationale for a decision—trust but verify. It may be a stray piece of information or a gut-feeling that is enough for a leader to spend a bit more time participating in a decision-making process.

Leadership author Jim Collins discusses the concept of holes in a boat in his book How the Mighty Fall. Holes above the waterline are damaging, but not critical. In those situations, trust can be more liberally applied. Yet, holes below the waterline are existential to the well-being of the boat and the crew, and a leader should consider the consequences carefully, spending more time as a part of decision-making processes when the stakes (and water) rise to that level. I vividly remember a situation where this concept came to life at Edwards when I was a squadron commander back in 2010.

FLASHBACK TO EDWARDS AFB (2010)

The next wing commander at Edwards was an F-22 pilot, and she rightfully wanted a Raptor as the backdrop for her incoming change of command. As a part of the ceremony, the official wing aircraft would have the wing commander's name painted under the left side of cockpit and be revealed for all to see as a part of the wing flagship. It was a magnificent part of the event.

Early in the morning of the event, the F-22 was positioned in the perfect place so that the name could be revealed and seen during the ceremony. On my drive in to work on that morning, I had one of those leader intuition moments when I literally felt the hair stand up on the back of my neck. The F-22 could be positioned in two different orientations, one where the left side of the cockpit was visible to the crowd and one where it was not. What a horrible, below-the-waterline moment it would be in the ceremony if it was time to reveal the wing commander's name and it couldn't be seen by the crowd.

I called my F-22 maintenance lead, Russ Deering, and asked him to check the orientation of the aircraft, a very uncharacteristic detail for me to concern myself with within a culture of trust that had developed in that organization. He laughed a bit at my request, assured me that it was likely oriented properly but was happy to double check on it. He called back a few minutes later, horrified to witness a jet that was turned the wrong way. The team quickly fixed it—no harm, no foul—but it did provide a good reminder that even

> the highly-trusted, most-capable teams require a bit of verification when the conditions are right and a leader's intuition suggests that something might be off when the stakes are high.

The Hustle Squad was thriving in their innovation and culture shaping activities. They were using all forms of communication to highlight the status of the campaign and telegraph progress. They created a fun and slick media campaign using social media to the maximum extent possible. After conspiring with AFWERX, they even rolled out a hashtag—#innovativeAF—to use extensively at Edwards as a part of our campaign. I was tracking their information flow and saw it was resonating well with our workforce who had truly started to define themselves as a part of a cutting-edge innovation movement. Additionally, our progress was catching the attention of Air Force Senior Leaders, and our Chief of Staff even retweeted one of our posts. Our stock was booming!

A member of our team made an off-hand comment to me after the Chief of Staff retweet about the use of #innovativeAF. Up to that point, as a member of an older generation, I assumed that the AF meant Air Force. It did, of course, but it also had another meaning that was a bit crass for my taste, though an accurate reflection of the magnitude of our movement. Not only were we liberally using #innovativeAF in our official media, but the leadership of the Air Force was now using it in their support of us and they were probably as clueless as I was in doing so.

This ended up being a non-event, but it gave me the opportunity to discuss an important lesson with the Hustle Squad. I fully trusted them and did not want to distract them from their impressive, unleashed progress through OSS-style self-sabotage. I also didn't want to dampen their enthusiasm. Yet, in their activities with more elevated-risk or higher visibility, I simply asked them to keep me in the loop ahead of time, so that I would not be surprised and could ultimately redirect something that might be beyond our collective comfort levels. In the end, our hashtag became a bit of a joke. Every time I would talk about #innovativeAF, I would add "AF means Air Force, of course." At least to me it did.

ACTION ITEMS

Action Item 1: Eliminate onerous decision-making and approval processes that sabotage the effectiveness and well-being of your organization.

Action Item 2: Structure approval processes so that a decision is pushed no lower than the position that can take responsibility for the full consequences of a decision and no higher than the position that is fully informed as a regular part of a leader's duties.

Action Item 3: Make "What do you recommend?" your favorite question to the experts in your trust-filled organization.

Action Item 4: Have the courage to trust! It is the lubricant of progress and the catalyst of communication in an organization.

Action Item 5: Spend more time as a part of decision-making processes when a decision is existential to the well-being of an organization—trust but verify based on the risk level of the decision and a leader's intuition.

Action Item 6: Encourage proactive communication from subordinates. It can cement the bonds of trust in your organization.

CHAPTER TEN

SPIKES ON A WIRE

In 2010, *Smithsonian Magazine* published, "Ten Inventions That Inadvertently Transformed Warfare," a thought-provoking essay written by Mark Strauss, an experienced science correspondent, author, and editor. As expected, Strauss's list contained several elaborate, complex transformational creations, like the locomotive, steamship, camera, and telegraph. These items had all begun as peacetime inventions that were quickly and naturally transitioned into military applications. Interestingly, the first two listed items were inventions that were extremely and shockingly simple: barbed wire and the bayonet.

Barbed wire was originally designed for agricultural use to contain livestock. It was quickly adopted by the military in recognition of its significant security applications. According to a World War I era U.S. Army publication, the barbed wire yielded unique defensive advantages because it was easily and quickly made, difficult to destroy, difficult to maneuver through, and offered no obstruction to defensive activity.

Impressive! In its reductionist form, though, barbed wire is simply a wire with spikes on it; nothing more, nothing less. Yet, it played a major role in shaping the conduct of warfare from the moment it was created.

Bayonets were originally adopted as a sporting improvement to provide protection for game hunters as they sought to subdue their dangerous prey. In the military application, bayonets allowed riflemen to protect themselves and others during the act of the rifle reloading, proving a potent force for success in close combat and becoming both a practical and psychological weapon. Much like the simplicity of the barbed wire, in its reductionist form the bayonet was just a gun with a knife strapped to the end of the barrel. It was an extremely basic concept that has also played a substantial role in both the historical and current conduct of warfare.

It is easy to conflate invention with innovation. The two items previously described were, in fact, invented but, more accurately, they were innovated. They weren't the result of a complex and expensive invention mechanism. Their creation didn't consume massive resources, nor did they require an excessive amount of time to conceptualize and create. The brightest minds didn't assemble to form and lead teams to bring these items into existence. They weren't part of a project that anyone would consider a moon-shot nor were they the product of an activity that would earn the flashy moniker of warp-speed. They were not the output of brilliant invention juggernauts like Jobs, Carver or Edison.

Instead, they were simple items that were conceptualized or combined in novel or unique ways to produce oversized outcomes. They were not new so much as they were new ways to use old things. Importantly, their creation was within the grasp of mere mortals without impressive specialty degrees, the backing of mountains of venture capital, or the massive economies of scale of large organizations. Yet, their return on investment was off the charts.

As the Hustle Squad started consolidating and considering the plethora of good ideas submitted by the Edwards workforce during our first innovation campaign in early 2019, they faced the daunting challenge of deciding which ideas to pursue and which to put on hold. It was a resourcing challenge as much as a socialization and messaging challenge.

CHAPTER TEN ♣ SPIKES ON A WIRE | 99

After all, the decisions made here would telegraph how serious our organization was in fully *listening, considering,* and *acting* to all the ideas submitted by our amazing workforce. The population at The Center of the Aerospace Testing Universe was waiting and watching to see how we would handle this challenge. Our innovation credibility was at stake.

As the Hustle Squad and Senior Innovation Council poured over the crowdsourced comments and votes for each idea, they came to an interesting and compelling conclusion—the best use of our allocated resources was to fund the largest number of potentially feasible ideas. With a few carefully selected exceptions, that meant that we were intentionally optimizing our resources to maximize the scope of impact as compared to the depth of impact. Essentially, we were pursuing bayonets and barbed wire instead of locomotives and steamships.

There were some important reasons for doing so that are not necessarily obvious. This construct allowed the team to pursue the largest number of submissions and connect with the greatest number of idea champions (i.e., those who submitted ideas). Doing so meant that more ideas would successfully transition to the act portion of the *listen, consider,* and *act* cycle. Thus, we incorporated more individuals into our innovation ecosystem by nature of the active pursuit of their ideas. It was an exercise in the creation of something advertising and behavioral science mastermind, Rory Sutherland, calls a *psychological moonshot*. We were creating a change of perception at scale and igniting a social contagion of employee engagement to supercharge the *listen, consider* and *act* cycle.

Sutherland tells us that "it seems likely that the biggest progress in the next 50 years may come not from improvements in technology but in psychology and design thinking. Put simply, it's easy to achieve massive improvements in *perception* at a fraction of the cost of equivalent improvements in *reality*. Logic tends to rule out magical improvements of this kind, but psycho-logic doesn't."

As a part of our psychological moonshot mindset, there were several avenues of innovation through the ideas that had been submitted. Sometimes the ideas were simple process changes. Sometimes they solved problems or irritants in the workforce with a policy waiver or a delegation of authority. Other times, they involved the application of existing equipment in different ways or unique combinations. These types of concepts often cost nothing financially. Thus, their return on investment is infinite.

Occasionally, an idea would incorporate an off-the-shelf item used outside the military to solve our military-related problems. In these cases, our pursuits were the best reflection of the concepts of the bayonet and barbed wire.

An important point, with respect to the selected ideas, is that the Hustle Squad was not responsible for the *act* phase. Instead, the idea champion was now to become the idea owner, and the ultimate success of the idea would hinge on their commitment to bringing it to fruition. They wouldn't do so alone, of course. They had financial support from our pool of innovation resources and the top-cover of leadership. They also had the mentoring commitment of the Hustle Squad, which came with additional training and education resources to help these idea owners become more skilled innovators. Thus, each new idea owner could use their experience and skills in maturing and implementing their immediate idea from this innovation campaign as a springboard for future innovation activity. As a result, this campaign enhanced the long-term cultural transformational goals of our organization beyond the immediate outcomes of the current ideas.

The pursuit of the simpler ideas had additional impacts that magnified the utility of this strategy. With more ideas and more idea owners involved in the *act* phase, there were more opportunities to publicize the progress of our innovation journey. Additionally, because these ideas were often easier to bring to fruition, it meant that there would be more and faster successes, which was also a boost to our robust public affairs methods and relentless socialization efforts. Follow through opportunities were extensive, and while we tried our best to get the word out about each idea and every success, I thought we could have highlighted our follow through with more fanfare than we did.

Ultimately though, the campaign was wildly successful in the many ways it impacted our workforce and mission. We saw successes in solar powered equipment on the flightline, the incorporation of unmanned systems to inspect our water pipes, increased recycle and reuse opportunities in our cafeteria, and improved options for on-base transportation. We even opened a new on-base restaurant, Wing Stop, and while physical fitness scores may have taken a short term hit with the infusion of buffalo wings into our diet, workforce morale soared!

There were also advantages to the ideas that fell below the cutline of our innovation campaign. Importantly, we never said no to ideas, rather simply said *not right now* or *not at the idea's current level of maturity*. This philosophical construct meant that we left the door open to all those who had submitted ideas and welcomed these idea champions with open arms as a key part of our broader innovation community. These idea champions also had the benefits of active mentorship from the Hustle Squad and were able to utilize additional innovation training and education resources that we identified for our committed innovators. Thus, we were able to add these idea champions to the rolls of our growing innovation ecosystem that would spread the word about our progress throughout The Center of the Aerospace Testing Universe.

These idea champions had more time to restructure or mature their ideas for future campaigns, and several of those ideas went on to eventually earn their rightful position in the *act* phase. As an example, an idea that originally did not transition to the *act* phase was matured and brought to life in a future campaign, improving safety on the flightline by incorporating new fall protection equipment for aircraft maintenance personnel.

Some of the larger, more expensive ideas that would have consumed our innovation support and financial resources had the great potential for long-term and wide-spread success. These idea owners were also incorporated into the innovation ecosystem, and we worked with them to find sponsors outside our immediate base community at Edwards. Sometimes, that meant these owners would submit their ideas as part of Air Force wide innovation campaigns or lobby AFWERX to consider adopting an idea by allocating their resources to its pursuit.

We would also work with idea champions to submit their ideas as concepts through the established funding streams of functional components within the Air Force (like civil engineering or aircraft maintenance) or through program offices that managed the development and sustainment of weapon systems (like F-16s and F-35s). We found ways to spend OPM—Other People's Money—my personal favorite TLA (three letter acronym)!

As an example of our success in this way, we experimented with an autonomous vehicle fleet for our on-base electronic warfare and bombing range complex to meet customer needs during flight testing. While that particular idea didn't reach large-scale success, it spurred several other capabilities at the range complex, successfully pulling it into the twenty-first century.

There is an urban legend about a strategy the United States Air Force uses to construct its bases. The concept originates from the notable fact that Air Force installations tend to have a well-earned reputation for being the nicest among the military services. When an Air Force construction project starts, everything is carefully designed and planned through a team of world class military civil engineers. Following that, the Air Force starts spending its construction resources on roads, office buildings, support facilities, housing, and even golf courses. Then it builds the hangars and aircraft maintenance facilities that will support the primary mission of the base. Lastly, it builds the base's runways.

This approach is simple but brilliant. The most important part of the base is its runways, without which, the base isn't actually a base. If overall construction funds allocated for the project are spent before the runways are completed, it will be an easy process to lobby for more resources because the argument is iron-clad that the base needs its runways. Thus, the overall size of the budget of the construction project will increase because OPM will be in plenteous supply when the operational flying capabilities of a new base hang in the balance.

Now, I don't actually believe that the Air Force intentionally uses such a strategy in the construction and resourcing of its bases, but there is wisdom in using this same concept with respect to a portfolio of ideas for innovation. For those whose impacts are cross-cutting and far-reaching, there are likely other sponsors in the broader organizational enterprise who can help with resourcing because of the direct applicability of that idea to meeting their requirements.

Tapping into those resources, especially as a volunteer springboard for an innovative process, novel concept, or beta test for a new piece of equipment broadens the ultimate pool of innovation activities through the magical use of OPM instead of consuming sparse internal resources. This concept enhanced the expanse and magnitude of our overall resource pool, allowing us to pursue 38 additional innovation projects with 42 million dollars of OPM.

A focus on the pursuit of the easier, less-costly ideas enjoyed additional benefits during the innovation campaign at Edwards. Our broad portfolio meant a multiplicative effect of the improvements on our base, mission, and quality of life. A small fix here and a marginal improvement there added up quickly. These wins began to touch every corner of the base and each member of our team. Bit-by-bit, improvement-by-improvement, innovative ideas started providing a cumulative and compounding practical benefit. Yet, these additive successes also facilitated cumulative, compounding cultural success as well. This strategy of prioritizing the easier ideas allowed us to gain momentum and demonstrate credibility. The return on investment, much like bayonets and barbed wire, was off the charts. It was like a snowball rolling down a mountain—getting bigger and faster with every successful rotation.

A critical corollary to the concepts just outlined is that the biggest budgets do not automatically yield the most substantial successes, nor do they produce the greatest innovative activity. Similarly, those who have the most resources to throw at problems do not always discover the most magnificent solutions.

> A perfect example of the best innovative activity to come from a small budget is the fierce competition in the early twentieth century between Samuel Langley and Orville and Wilbur Wright. It was characterized as a bitter feud that lingered on through institutional

inertia until 1942 when the Smithsonian Institution finally had to acknowledge the Wright Brothers' success in achieving the first flight nearly 40 years prior. Langley had lost, and the Smithsonian wasn't happy about it.

Samuel Langley was the third secretary of the Smithsonian Institution, a position largely considered as our nation's chief scientist at the time. As it is today, the Smithsonian is a massive organization bankrolled by the U.S. Government. Langley, using the institutional resources at his disposal, was committed to winning the race to successfully create and operate the first heavier-than-air machine in powered flight, fully expecting to fly the first airplane in human history. He was right to think he would do so because his only apparent competition was a couple of newspaper printers turned bicycle tinkers from Dayton, Ohio known as the Wright Brothers.

While Langley was arrogantly spending money by leaping into the air and testing his concepts, the duo from Dayton were carefully and miserly considering various concepts for success as they marched through innovative concepts that would inform every component of powered flight.

The Wright Brothers were a savvy duo without deep pockets. Committed to their cause, they went about systematically considering the challenges set before them. They watched and studied birds, flew kites and gliders, and carefully explored creative concepts, such as wing warping, propeller design, airfoil optimization, and control system configuration. They even created a wind tunnel to methodically test and evaluate their novel ideas, filling volumes of notebooks with their findings.

In the end, Samuel Langley nearly died by throwing himself and his resources into his failed attempts at flight. On the other hand, the Wright Brothers succeeded in conducting four flights on a gusty day in Kittyhawk, North Carolina on December 17, 1903. In his failed pursuits, Langley was bankrolled with over $70,000 in investments (about two million dollars in today's dollars), while the Wright Brothers only spent $1,000 (about $28,000 in today's dollars).

CHAPTER TEN ♣ SPIKES ON A WIRE | 105

The investment of Orville and Wilbur was less than two percent of that of Langley, yet it yielded a massive return. It also demonstrated an important example that the biggest budget does not always yield the most bang for the innovation buck. Magnificent results can stem from modest investments, whether in North Carolina in 1903 or Iraq in 2020.

FLASHFORWARD TO IRAQ (2020-2021)

As discussed in the previous chapter, my deployment to Iraq as our nation's Senior Defense Official and Defense Attaché was a tense one because of the destructive activities of the Iranian-aligned militia groups active in the country. At the end of 2020, the threats from these groups had become so credible and severe that the United States was on the verge of a full-scale evacuation and closure of the Embassy in Baghdad on the direction of Secretary of State Mike Pompeo. Other nations would have quickly followed the United States in its exit from the country, and the entire international diplomatic presence and credibility of the Iraqi Government hung in the balance. The situation was dire, and the ramifications had a global impact.

Into the breach stepped a young Army Major and artillery officer named Jeb Graydon. Following the evacuation of the majority of our team to Kuwait, he was the only security cooperation case officer that remained in Baghdad based on the strict personnel limitations because of the extreme threat at the time. As a member of my team, Jeb devised novel concepts to successfully secure the International Zone (IZ), thus meeting the security requirements of the diplomatic community and bolstering the resolve and credibility of the Iraqi Government.

It all started with Jeb rapidly creating an American-funded contract to survey the situation in the IZ. This survey team arrived in Baghdad at a pivotal moment when things seemed to be collapsing. Their directive was simple: assess security conditions of the IZ, establish reasonable requirements to resolve concerns, and create short- and long-term plans to implement recommendations. Meanwhile, Jeb cobbled together our organizational resources and other sources of funding (OPM) to demonstrate the American commitment to the security needs of the IZ. He found excess U.S. military vehicles in the Middle East that could be divested to the Iraqi military and police for security patrols, identified sources of protective gear for Iraqi security personnel, and found unused concrete barriers and barbed wire that could be relocated into the heart of Baghdad.

Almost immediately, things changed in the Iraqi capital, even though the only tangible manifestation of Jeb's activities at the time was the conduct of a simple security survey and the creation of a plan to reallocate and redirect existing resources. Security concerns started to wane. The Government of Iraq began to demonstrate courage, commitment, and resolve in their duties to protect the international diplomatic contingent in their capital city. And ultimately, the United States backed down from its threat to remove its diplomatic presence, convinced that the situation had stabilized by the new-found resolve of the Iraqi security apparatus. Literally, a quick-thinking and unleashed Major, a bit of barbed wire and a few other simple acts of creative thinking saved the day. Meager investments in innovation yielded massive returns. Mark Strauss and the Smithsonian Magazine would have been proud!

ACTION ITEMS

Action Item 1: Don't confuse innovation and invention. Innovation is not primarily about creating new things. Instead, it is more about creating new ways to use old things. Thus, innovative activity can have a return on investment that is massive because its costs can be minimal.

Action Item 2: Strongly consider intentionally optimizing resources to maximize the scope of impact instead of the depth of impact.

Action Item 3: Employ the powerful concepts of psychological moonshots.

Action Item 4: Mentor and support innovators with institutional resources.

Action Item 5: Fund ideas through OPM (Other People's Money), whenever possible.

CHAPTER ELEVEN

A MESSAGE IN THE MISFORTUNES

Supreme Court Chief Justice John Roberts was asked to give the commencement address at the Cardigan Mountain School's ninth-grade graduation in 2016. This type of a ceremony would not normally rise to the level of such a distinguished speaker, but since his son was a graduate to be honored at the event, Chief Justice Roberts graciously accepted. His words were novel and thought-provoking, largely because they were atypical for such an event that is usually filled with predictable praise and platitudes. The following is a portion of what he said on that day:

"Now the commencement speakers will typically also wish you good luck and extend good wishes to you. I will not do that, and I'll tell you why. From time to time in the years to come, I hope you will be treated unfairly, so that you will come to know the value of justice. I hope that you will suffer betrayal because that will teach you the importance of loyalty. Sorry to say, but I hope you will be lonely from time to time so that you don't take friends for granted. I wish you bad luck, again, from time to time so that you will be conscious of the role of chance in life and understand that your success is not completely deserved, and that the failure of others is not completely deserved either. And when you lose, as you will from time to time, I hope every now and then, your opponent will gloat over your failure. It is a way for you to understand the importance of sportsmanship. I hope you'll be ignored so you know the importance of listening to others, and I hope you will have just enough pain to learn compassion. Whether I wish these things or not, they're going to happen. And whether you benefit from them or not will depend upon your ability to see the message in your misfortunes."

These widely covered statements were remarkable. Roberts purposefully wished for those ninth-grade boys to have a future pocked with occasional unfair treatment, betrayal, loneliness, bad luck, poor sportsmanship, neglect, and pain. For each of these natural occurrences of the negative side of life, there would be a lesson to learn, so the boys would grow, improve and gain perspective. They would glean invaluable truths about justice, loyalty, friendship, proportionality, good sportsmanship, sensitivity, and compassion. Chief Justice Roberts reminded them that there is an important message in the inevitable misfortunes of life.

In 1914, Thomas Edison's large industrial facility in New Jersey was ravaged by an explosion and consumed by a substantial fire. Famously, Edison told his son Charles, "Go get your mother and all her friends. They'll never see a fire like this again … We've just got rid of a lot of rubbish."

In the early 1940s, an IBM Corporation employee was assigned the responsibility of securing a million-dollar deal. He failed in his bid and offered to resign. Thomas Watson, IBM CEO, responded, "Fire you? I just invested one million dollars in your education. Why would I fire you?"

For Edison, even in a disastrous fire there was something to learn and appreciate. For Watson, even in a costly blown deal there was something to glean and an opportunity to grow.

CHAPTER ELEVEN ♣ A MESSAGE IN THE MISFORTUNES

Runner, coach, and mentor Steve Magness writes about his extensive research on toughness in *Do Hard Things*. He says that "real toughness is experiencing discomfort or distress, leaning in, paying attention, and creating space to take thoughtful action. It's maintaining a clear head to be able to make the appropriate decision. Toughness is navigating discomfort to make the best decision you can. And research shows that this model of toughness is more effective at getting results than the old one." He goes on to say that "research consistently shows that tougher individuals are able to perceive stressful situations as challenges instead of threats." According to Magness, challenges should generally be seen as opportunities, not threats.

Dr Carol Dweck, Stanford University Professor of Psychology, discusses the two fundamental mindsets available to all of us: a fixed or growth mindset. Fixed mindsets are characterized by a fear of failure and an avoidance of challenges. This mindset yields paralysis and stagnation. Growth mindsets are characterized by persistence in the face of failure, a love of learning, and a willingness to embrace challenges. This mindset produces lifelong, enduring opportunities for improvement. The former sees a failure as a permanent feature that halts progress, while the latter sees a failure as a temporary setback that can prompt forward progress. In the former, failure is to be avoided at all costs. In the latter, failure is an inevitable feature of continuous improvement. According to Dweck, challenges actually create opportunities.

Leaders must carefully and deliberately guide the response of their organization to the inevitable onslaught of shortcomings and failures, which there *will* be.

To paraphrase Chief Justice Roberts—Failure is going to happen whether we like it or not. It is a natural part of life and can actually be a catalyst for growth. The way we handle success and failure will largely determine whether our future is characterized by progressive growth or fixed stagnation.

A leader's proper response to bad news or failure can quickly transmit a willingness to embrace the opportunity in every challenge. On the other hand, a single negative overreaction can sour the organizational culture such that it eliminates any willingness to absorb risk that could generate opportunities for progress. Such a risk-adverse culture halts the progress of organizational transformation and innovation, which can only be painstakingly reversed over time, if at all.

Leaders can set the right tone to establish the foundation for a growth mindset instead of a fixed mindset. Those leaders who gracefully accept naturally occurring failures recognize the important message in the inevitable misfortunes of life. Even in these situations, there is something to learn and appreciate. The threats are mere challenges that may actually be catalysts for progress. As Winston Churchill once said, "Success consists of going from failure to failure without loss of enthusiasm."

At The Center of the Aerospace Testing Universe, we wanted to harness these important truths to further our innovation journey and cultural transformation. During the Hustle Squad consideration, prioritization, and triage of all the submitted ideas, several did not meet our criteria for resourcing and action at this stage of the innovation campaign. Those ideas might be considered failures, and we realized that how we treated them and, more importantly, the idea champions would say a lot about our actual culture. In fact, how we handled those so-called failures would impact our workforce more than how we handled the successes. As a result, we chose to deliberately celebrate those who had the courage to contribute ideas that were ultimately not selected, and *Dunkin with Dragon* was born.

We only had a single Dunkin' Donuts in the Aerospace Valley, about 30 minutes south in Lancaster, California. While I'm not particularly fond of donuts of any brand, I think that the coffee at Dunkin' is world-class. Thus, creating an event that included coffee and donuts seemed like a win for the donut-lovers and coffee-lovers alike. It also gave me an excuse to import a Box-of-Joe from the Dunkin' in Lancaster.

The venue for Dunkin with Dragon was the massive wrap-around balcony on the third floor of the wing headquarters building, overlooking the flightline at Edwards. The desert environment creates a windy climate, especially on an elevated structure, but the balcony location is unmatched in its view of the activities on the robust Edwards' flight

CHAPTER ELEVEN ♣ A MESSAGE IN THE MISFORTUNES

schedule, making it is easy to overlook the strong breeze. For Dunkin with Dragon, we carefully selected an exclusive guest list to communicate an important point to those who were still sizing up our commitment to *listen, consider,* and *act.*

This great event was hosted by me, the Hustle Squad, and the Senior Innovation Council. Our guests of honor were all idea champions whose ideas were not selected as a part of our original innovation campaign. In a different world, they could be considered failures, but we chose to flip the script by showing our appreciation to those who had trusted us with their ideas. We celebrated and assured them that the next innovation campaign would give them a chance to make follow-on submissions.

Together, we enjoyed donuts, coffee, and fellowship. The innovation leadership team invested our time in these key members of our workforce, and through the strategic use of our schedules, we celebrated progress disguised as failure. In addition to the key strategic messaging that emphasized our recognition of the opportunities in the midst of challenges, there were some additional, unexpected benefits in creating such a venue.

Resulting from Dunkin with Dragon, these idea champions got to rub shoulders with one another. While the idea owners were working with the Hustle Squad to bring their suggestions to fruition, these budding innovators were building relationships, thus creating an additional component of our innovation ecosystem. Through the casual conversation over coffee and donuts, the innovation leadership team was able to provide some informal mentorship about the "failed" idea submissions and innovative concepts that would yield better, subsequent submissions in future campaigns.

Additionally, as we discussed ideas while watching the daily ad hoc airshow, we discovered that some of these "failed" ideas could be combined, based on their similarities with one another, to make something more potent and compelling. It was even the case that a few of the idea champions sculpted their ideas so quickly and effectively as a result of the discussions on that day, that when innovation resources were freed up, they were poised to secure a spot on the success list. Thus, we saw real examples of challenges that yielded opportunities. However,

Dunkin with Dragon was only one way we celebrated failures during our innovation journey.

At times, progress faces opposition from outside the organization. It might be by a resistant boss or bureaucratic quicksand. The opposition that hurts the most, however, is that which comes from inside an organization. It is like an act of intentional cultural sabotage that would make the World War II-era OSS proud.

As mentioned in Chapter 8, we gave out a variety of swag, including t-shirts, during the pep rally kickoff of our innovation campaign. Our friends at The Gapingvoid Culture Design Group created a great logo for the shirts and mascot for our campaign, which were emblazoned with the phrase "This is a Movement" and our #innovativeAF hashtag (AF means Air Force). But not everyone appreciated the pep rally swag.

An individual from our workforce filed a formal, anonymous complaint about a misuse of government funds in purchasing the shirts. Though we had properly contracted this expenditure while consulting with the experts to ensure that we were on the right side of law and policy, facing such a complaint could take the wind out of anyone's sails. It also risked promoting a culture of caution that would be a regressive force in our innovation movement.

We endured the investigation and were vindicated by the outcome. In order to celebrate the hardships that come from such situations and the uneven pace of progress, we created a secret innovation society that included a slightly modified t-shirt oozing with subtle sarcasm. I personally inducted the secret society members by giving this revised shirt to those who had substantial scars caused by our innovation battles. It was deliberately designed to reward toughness and remind the heartiest of innovators that we appreciated them in spite of the wounds caused by their detractors and our organizational saboteurs. The secret society provided an important message during incidents of misfortune while also celebrating a chance to reinforce the lean-in toughness of our innovation team.

Challenges come in all shapes and sizes. One of the biggest organizational efforts in the flight test world comes with the preparation for the initial

CHAPTER ELEVEN ♣ A MESSAGE IN THE MISFORTUNES | 115

testing of a new aircraft. The next first-flight on our schedule at Edwards was for the Air Force's new trainer aircraft, the T-7 Red Hawk. Such a milestone requires planning for facilities, support equipment, test instrumentation, maintenance activities, test structure, safety protocols, and flight scheduling.

Based on the ideal conditions and expertise at The Center of the Aerospace Testing Universe, the execution of testing is normally accomplished onsite at Edwards, but the contractor, in this case, wanted to perform the bulk of the early testing at their facilities and airspace near their final assembly location in St Louis, Missouri. We were rightfully concerned that this created conditions that would bypass proper government oversight of such an important new part of the Air Force fleet. The contractor, however, made a strong case for the financial and schedule benefits of retaining their home court advantage, and the program office seemed convinced by their enticing logic.

Virtually, we sparred with the contractor and program office over the test-location decision. They had combined forces against the test professionals and were poised to solidify a decision that we knew was unwise. As a result of the standoff, the government leader from the program office made a visit to Edwards to explain how our thinking was outdated and un innovative. How dare someone say that about us!

We were ready for this challenge. We planned the visit to give the program office leader a comprehensive view of flight test and explain the major benefits of onsite testing and the necessity of government-led flight testing to provide proper oversight for a new program. We also scheduled the visit to emphasize our innovative culture and transformation journey. Most importantly, we were ready to offer the ace up our sleeve, a newly-created innovative concept, when we eventually heard the line, "You might have some impressive innovation wins at Edwards, but you are stuck in old thinking when it comes to T-7 testing."

Our test range experts had created a novel concept that allowed for much of the testing to be conducted in St Louis but executed remotely from Edwards via fiber optic cables that linked the Midwest with the Mojave Desert. There were some concerns with latency of data transmission during real-time test conduct, but the team created a checkout process to build the data linkages and verify that the transmission delays were acceptably small. This construct would provide all the benefits the contractor and government program office were clamoring for, with the expertise and oversight needed by the government and test professionals to ensure the Air Force would receive a trainer that had been rigorously tested and evaluated.

It was a brilliant idea proving that our innovation culture powerfully extended to all areas of our mission. It also completely flipped the script of the visit and quickly reversed the false narrative that it was the Edwards team stuck in the past, creating a two-fold opportunity in the midst of a seemingly substantial challenge.

Sometimes, however, leaders need to be even more explicit in the messaging on the value of toughness to their teams.

Senior Airman Oscar Cantu was an Air Traffic Controller at Edwards with a vision that would assist the mission through augmented reality tools. This vision would provide better situational awareness in the challenging conditions of air traffic control during busy flying operations, bad weather, or visual limitations of the control tower's configuration. Yet, his well-reasoned concept faced several detractors and few advocates. Cantu persevered through the obstacles and adversity, refusing to give up on his creative idea and the improvements he knew would naturally flow from this concept.

Our innovation leaders felt like we needed to recognize Senior Airman Cantu for his willingness to face frequent obstacles in the pursuit of opportunities. As a result, he became the inaugural winner of the Grit Award—a publicized award for those whose innovation journey required remarkable persistence and resilience. It was an opportunity to create a culture where awards were not only given for serendipitous successes, but also for well-reasoned failures, especially when pursued with grit.

The Edwards workforce learned a powerful lesson as a result of his experience. Upon accepting his award, Cantu said, "The Grit Award was presented to me because of the challenges I have faced so far with my innovation idea that I am very passionate about. However, despite these difficulties and setbacks, I pushed through to make my dream become a reality no matter what it took." Cantu was characterized by the type of toughness described by Steve Magness, turning challenges into opportunities. He leaned into the resistance he faced and made space for sanity to prevail, which ultimately led to a resourced pursuit of his idea. It wasn't easy; it required grit.

It is not only the lower levels of the workforce that will face shortcomings in pursuit of innovation. Senior leaders fail as well, and the grit demonstrated by Senior Airman Cantu must be embraced by leaders across the chain of command. When leaders demonstrate toughness and grit in the pursuit of the right causes, even when an idea ultimately fails, it powerfully conveys the importance of the concepts previously described to the rest of the organization.

In my case, we faced a long-term battle advocating for a great idea that never gained the traction we expected. At The Center of the Aerospace Testing Universe, we lacked sufficient on-base housing for our population. Our remote location meant that our workforce would either be able to live on base or face long commutes and weighty challenges finding housing in the expensive environment of Southern California. The average wait time for an on-base house was nearly a year, forcing members of our team to find semi-permanent housing off base for several months as they waited. In addition to solving the supply and demand problem, more housing would yield a larger on-base resident population, allowing us to scale up educational and recreational offerings there as well. It would be a win-win.

In conjunction with our on-base housing contractor, we crafted a creative solution to this shortfall—building an on-base apartment complex for families. This had never been done in the Department of Defense, and the initial capital expenditures and risks would be absorbed by the contractor who would build and operate the apartments. Yet, the bureaucratic approval process consumed days, weeks, months, and years as our population continued enduring the burdens of long commutes and unsafe, expensive off-base neighborhoods.

In advocating for progress on this project, I discussed it with leaders at all levels in the military, community, and even Congress. Everyone seemed to believe that it was a great idea, but the system couldn't quite get around the structural impediments to bring it to fruition. During my last few days as the commander at Edwards, I reached out again to the key leaders that could help us get to yes. Yet, the project languished, and several years later, it is still working its way at a plodding pace through the approval system.

I wish that I could share the Hollywood ending to this saga, but it would have to be written as a fictional account. It doesn't, however, mean that it wasn't a worthy cause, it just means that it isn't over, the final chapter of that story is not yet written. And while the idea could be considered a failure based on its current status, uneven success is a part of the natural process of progress. Not everything works out, even with the grit, toughness, and creativity that comes with an innovative organizational culture. It happens to idea champions at all levels, and a few losses at the wing commander level simply provided an important message to the entire team about the inevitable misfortunes or uneven progress in the pursuit of organizational improvement and transformation. Chief Justice Roberts and the ninth-grade boys from the Cardigan Mountain School would completely understand.

ACTION ITEMS

Action Item 1: Do not overreact to shortcomings or failures, or you risk undermining future progress and silencing the *listen, consider,* and *act* process.

Action Item 2: Find creative ways to celebrate successes and *failures,* because both are key components of organizational progress.

Action Item 3: Seize the opportunities that accompany challenges, and even award and publicize them.

CHAPTER TWELVE

TRIAL BY DRAGON

Abolitionist and woman's suffragist Frederick Douglass was known as one of the best communicators in the latter half of the nineteenth century. His words were a powerful reminder of the key principles of liberty and the stark tragedy of the tyranny of slavery. As an escaped slave from Maryland, Douglass fully understood the tragic nature of the institution of slavery and its costly impact on individuals, families, and society. He also understood the power of theater and employed a fanciful style to capture the attention of audiences and convey the power of his message.

He once said, "I shall endeavor not to forget that people do not attend lectures to hear statesmanlike addresses, which are usually rather heavy for the stomachs of young and old who listen. People want to be amused as well as instructed. They come as often for the former as the latter, and perhaps as often to see the man as for either." In the end, he knew that his important cause would be furthered by a bit of showiness.

While we did face the occasional setback during our innovation journey, we saw more progress than pessimism at The Center of the Aerospace Testing Universe. Importantly, our movement was resonating with the workforce, and the *listen, consider,* and *act* cycle was in full swing. We were also finding ways to have a bit of fun, and the enthusiasm was feeding upon itself.

In Chapters 3 and 6, I made negative references to the phrase *innovation theater*. In other situations around the Air Force, we'd seen activity that portended a serious commitment to innovative cultural change, but the actions were hollow. It was a backlot stage with no substance, a slight of hand with no real magic. Yet, while the use of the term *theater* conjures up negative reactions, there is nothing wrong with a bit of showiness. Along with our real progress, we were finding ways to keep the workforce interested and engaged as a multiplier to our efforts and having fun along the way.

From the outset of our journey at Edwards, like Douglass, we employed a bit of showiness ourselves. From innovation pep rallies to a TEDx event in our anechoic chamber to dad-joke-telling Commander's Calls to a Dunkin with Dragon on our wing headquarters balcony, we were keeping the workforce engaged and entertained with a bit of showmanship. It was fun, and it was fanciful. Most importantly, it was fulfilling our objective of keeping the momentum going for our innovation journey.

One of the showiest elements of our campaign was something we called Trial by Dragon in which a champion of an innovative idea was pitted against an expert who advocated for the status quo. There would be opening arguments, cross examinations, and closing arguments, and the base-wide workforce was encouraged to attend. While innovation was our intent, it did not mean that we favored the innovative if the prudent solution meant retaining the prevailing process or policy.

In order to be a proper judge, I needed a long flowing black robe, which we found alongside an essential gavel in our on-base courtroom. The powder grey wig that typified the litigation of yore, however, had to be obtained via the internet. When I wore it, I looked like a goof, but theater demanded that I fully play the part and embrace the character. At least it was better than wearing an elf costume.

During the event, we allocated time to a variety of arguments and cases. The Hustle Squad set the ground rules and enforced the timelines. The audience members enjoyed themselves, and I occasionally needed to call for *order in the court* while slamming my gavel on the table. The cases considered covered important mission-related and quality-of-life topics, and the debate was rich and entertaining. Both sides of all topics were well-prepared, making the decisions difficult at times. I tried my best to rule with authority and discernment, though I fell far short of the wisdom of Solomon.

At the end of the event, we opened the forum to questions from the audience, and one of the queries demanded a well-reasoned answer. Though simple, the question was profound—"What criteria was used to make my final determinations?" I'm glad that individual asked because, during the courtroom arguments, I was asking myself how I would justify my ruling in each case in front of the large audience.

As we went through the arguments, I created a decision-making rubric while listening to the particulars of each case. I explained my process and the criteria I considered. Frankly though, I should have considered this important question before the event began. My rubric consisted of:

- What problem are we solving?
- How does the new idea compare to foundational principles?
- What do designated experts think about the new idea?
- What are the risks and costs to implementing the new idea?
- What authorities are required to make the change?
- Is there some middle ground between the new idea and the status quo that is better than either?

Each of these considerations requires a bit of amplification and explanation.

What Problem Are We Solving?

As much as I love innovation, there is no reason to do something different if there is not an upside. New ideas are needed to solve problems. New ideas are also needed if they better meet an emerging or established requirement or changing condition. Importantly though, new is not always better, and change for change-sake is often more harmful than the status quo. Thus, any consideration of a new idea must start with the simple question, "Why do we need new?" To some extent, the status quo is innocent until proven guilty.

How Does the New Idea Compare to Foundational Principles?

Every organization has established values and foundational principles as does every individual, family, community, and society. These rest at the core of defining who we are and what we do. They are the bedrock of culture and organizational well-being. Unless the new idea is intended to deliberately alter the foundation, then it should be judged against the most basic parameters of the current one.

The strongest argument in favor of a new idea is that it allows the organization to better align with core values. The most damning argument is that it erodes an established foundation. It is a great risk to pursue a new idea when this most fundamental element of the decision-making matrix is not carefully and explicitly considered.

What Do Designated Experts Think About the New Idea?

In Chapter 7, I discussed the power of leadership wisdom and humility, and the core of this concept is a leader's commitment to involve subject matter experts in the decision-making process. This does not mean that a leader is yielding the responsibly and authority for the results of the decision to someone else, but it does mean that it is worth taking the time to consult experts before making a consequential decision. Admittedly, an expert is often the one most wedded to the status quo. After all, they are the ones most likely trapped by Thomas Kuhn's paradigm that has shaped their field of expertise and maximized an inertial influence. Yet, a leader owes it to themselves and their organization to consider the nuances of a decision informed by expert advice.

What Are the Risks and Costs to Implementing the New Idea?

The consideration of risk is understanding the benefits and downsides of change as the result of a new idea. Experts may be the ones most qualified to advise a leader on the negative ramifications of a change, and any consultation should explore this area of consideration.

Sometimes, there is a clear cost in time or resources to implement a change. These parameters should be known and weighed against the expected benefits of a new idea. A leader should also consider risk—financial, reputational, moral, operational, legal, safety, security—that yields a potential disadvantage to any change. Only then can a leader properly weigh the benefits with the costs and risks to make a proper decision.

What Authorities Are Required to Make the Change?

Even a senior level leader has boundaries of authority that limit their ability to support every change at their level. They may be constrained by a budget, laws or organizational policy or procedure. Their superiors may retain authority in this particular area at their higher levels instead of delegating it. None of this means a new idea is impossible, but the decision should reflect the authorities as they exist and those that require adjustment to bring a new idea to fruition.

One of my favorite Culture Wall tiles in the entryway of our wing headquarters stated, "If it's not a law, it's a suggestion." While appropriately provocative, it is not entirely accurate. There are authorities reflected in organizational policies and procedures that are more than mere suggestions, and a senior leader needs to understand the severe risk of recklessly disregarding these that may bring an abrupt end to a innovation journey. Nonetheless, there is always a waiver authority, and approval is typically easier than it first appears.

It is also true that laws have waiver authorities, which come in the form of new laws or legal loopholes. These are more difficult to maneuver through than getting beyond organizational policies and procedures, but, with the right partnership or support from a Congressional delegation, even these can be scalable obstacles. These topics will both be covered in the following chapter.

Is There Some Middle Ground Between the New Idea and the Status Quo That Is Better Than Either?

President Theodore Roosevelt once said, "It is never well to take drastic action if the results can be achieved with equal efficiency in less drastic fashion." Fortunately, life is not typically black or white. There is a lot of grey area in between decision-making extremes, all of which is fruitful maneuver room for a decision maker to consider.

In the balance between costs, benefits, and risks, there are many positions in the grey area that allow a decision maker to optimize their position far better than clinging to the status quo or accepting a new idea wholesale. There may be a fruitful opportunity for a trial run or experiment. There may also be a decision in that grey area that falls within the senior leader's authorities where a more polar solution does not. In that case, there's potential to satisfy all stakeholders and major factors of consideration.

TALK WITH TEAM TEICHERT

If the Edwards workforce didn't get to see me in the wig and judge's robe at our Trial by Dragon event, I also wore this attire as my Halloween costume that year. Hanging around my neck was an oversized necklace made up of my favorite Culture Wall tile—"Find out where 'no' lives and kill it." Although every event wasn't appropriate for such hilarity, there was still plenty of room for productive innovation theater. Sometimes, my family even participated in the fun.

We call our family *Team Teichert*. As a military family that moves frequently and needs a special bond to handle the unique challenges of our lifestyle, it seemed fitting to call us a team. This phrase also stems from one of my pet-peeves, which is when a military member thanks their family *for supporting them as they serve*. I feel such phrasing marginalizes the service and sacrifice of a military member's family. A better way to phrase such appreciation is to thank their family *for serving alongside of them*. After all, the military spouse and children play an important role in serving their country, even though they do not wear a uniform or take an oath. I have been proud to serve our great nation as a part of Team Teichert.

Some of my greatest memories of my time in the military are from serving alongside my amazing wife, Melonie, and our wonderful kids, Summer, Tiffany and Noah. I fondly remember going to military activities with them or using a military ceremony as a date night with my wife or one of my children. It brings a smile to my face to remember times serving meals at on-base dining halls to show our collective appreciation to the younger members of our team during the holidays. I fondly recall the many times we drove around our sprawling base on Thanksgiving, Christmas Eve, Christmas or New Years, visiting members whose positions required them to work on those days, delivering treats, small gifts, a firm handshake, a warm smile, a sincere thank you, and maybe even a dad joke or two.

One of my fondest memories is an event during the innovation journey at Edwards that we called *Talk with Team Teichert*, which was a chance for my family and me to sit on a stage and share our unfiltered, unrehearsed thoughts as a military family in our highly visible leadership role. I had never seen or heard about anyone doing this before, and I wanted to provide a candid, transparent venue to focus on military family issues as a part of our genuine care and concern for our population and provide extra thrust for our innovation and transformation voyage.

Talk with Team Teichert was held in front of a live audience and broadcasted to a virtual audience within the Edwards community as well as virtual audiences from around the world. It was recorded and posted online, and you can still watch it today. As I recently did so, I beamed with pride for my family. Other than my opening comments, that only lasted a few minutes, there were truly no planned remarks or preparation in the Teichert household.

Talk with Team Teichert was largely spent answering questions from the live and virtual audiences. It was an hour-and-a-half of honesty and authenticity that provided a glimpse into our lives and a chance for us to connect with the far-reaching community that was watching. My middle daughter Tiffany, a showman herself, had a microphone in her hand the entire time and wasn't afraid to use it. Melonie, Summer, and Noah also provided thoughtful and honest responses throughout the event. It was raw and live. It was magnificent, a further extension of the *listen, consider,* and *act* cycle that literally featured my amazing family using a visible and compelling platform.

THE INNOVATION SHOWCASE

During this period, the Edwards population also enjoyed a spectacle that we called the Innovation Showcase. While we had already enjoyed an open-door opportunity for our workforce to hear directly from innovators about their ideas on a small scale, this forum allowed us to take over our large on-base ballroom so innovators could pitch their ideas to a large crowd. The judge for this forum was the crowd itself, and their votes determined the outcome of our allocated innovation resources for this phase of the innovation movement.

The pitches from the Innovation Showcase were all informative, and those that were best received included a bit of theater in their presentations. The Hustle Squad had the bandwidth and resources to add a few of the new ideas from the showcase into our innovation portfolio, and one had truly knocked our socks off.

Lieutenant Colonel Raven "Rost" LeClair pitched Project FoX, which stands for Fighter Optimization eXperiment. This idea had the potential to revolutionize the modernization timeline, flexibility, and adaptability of our nation's cutting-edge aircraft.

Advanced aircraft are managed by software with millions of lines of code. In the traditional acquisition system, any software upgrade to an aircraft would be a carefully scheduled, pre-planned event, creating latency when adding the latest updates. That latency could be the difference between a successful combat engagement and one that ends with an American pilot hanging from a parachute over enemy territory after having their multi-million-dollar aircraft shot out from under them.

CHAPTER TWELVE ♠ **TRIAL BY DRAGON** | 127

The modernization software programs of these cutting-edge systems are unlike the regularly occurring cell phone upgrades that keep us current, secure, and fully functional. But why couldn't they be? That is what Project FoX aimed to find out.

This concept was simple but powerful. Using a tablet from the cockpit, a test pilot could tie directly into the aircraft's stream of software code to develop and employ real-time updates to solve tactical problems. If there was a certain frequency that was not being jammed properly by the electronic warfare systems, they could adjust the software through a new app to do so. If there was a radar system that was not accurately displaying the mix of targets, they could tweak the systems via a new app to improve the way the information was transmitted to the pilot.

In reality, software designers had been talking about *open system architecture* for years, but Project FoX was the ultimate manifestation of a long overdue concept. Pulling from a library of software applications, our cutting-edge aircraft could receive updates to their capabilities in days or weeks instead of months or years.

Rost's vision would bring this concept to life, and the audience at the Innovation Showcase recognized the magnitude of the potential impact. As he presented his idea, they cheered, heckled through good-natured fun, laughed, and, ultimately and overwhelmingly, supported his concept.

In about a year, Rost and his team tested Project FoX on an F-35 Lightning II while it operated on a taxiway on the ground in the Mojave Desert. Another year later, the Project FoX team was flying with this concept over the desert floor in an F-22 Raptor, causing the 4-star general of combat forces in the United States to say that this "initiative allows us to rapidly discover and iterate on combat capabilities and stay relevant with cutting-edge technology and affordably accelerate change in delivering combat Air Force capabilities as an enterprise."

Far removed from the cheers, good-natured heckles, laughs, and overwhelming support from the ballroom during the Innovation Showcase at Edwards, the American warfighter was now cheering as well. So were the families on base, who kickstarted a Spouse Innovation

Showcase, that further broadened the reach of the *listen, consider,* and *act* cycle.

With such success in mind, the fun and functionality of Trial by Dragon, Talk with Team Teichert, and Innovation Showcases allowed these events to be big successes and key components of our innovation journey at The Center of the Aerospace Testing Universe. They provided instruction, amusement, and warfighter impact. Frederick Douglass would have been proud of our theater with a purpose.

ACTION ITEMS

Action Item 1: Add an appropriate dose of showiness to your innovation methods to attract and maintain the attention of the workforce.

Action Item 2: Consider the following questions when deciding between a new idea or the status quo:

- What problem are we solving?
- How does the new idea compare to foundational principles?
- What do designated experts think about the new idea?
- What are the risks and costs to implementing the new idea?
- What authorities are required to make the change?
- Is there some middle ground between the new idea and the status quo that is better than either?

CHAPTER THIRTEEN

NON-MATERIAL SOLUTIONS

Chuck Yeager had been pulled from his Test Pilot School (TPS) class to be a part of the X-1 program and eventually became the pilot who first broke the sound barrier in that rocket plane. Shortly after the X-1 program finished, the rule-followers of the day made a point that Yeager was not qualified to be a test pilot because he had not fully finished the course at TPS. It was ridiculous to regress the record-shattering test pilot back to school, but the "rules are rules" mentality prevailed, and Yeager was sidelined until he could finish his remaining six-month chunk of schooling.

An extra hard workload was dumped on him by instructors who were jealous of his world-record-breaking accomplishments. Though his practical flight test experience had dwarfed the school curriculum, the antagonistic attitude of the instructors was overwhelming, especially when added to the extra responsibilities Yeager carried as an in-demand test pilot persona. The instructors ganged up on Yeager to try and fail him out, but Brigadier General Albert Boyd, commander of Edwards, stepped in, slammed his fist on the table and demanded the attention of the TPS commandant. In that meeting, Boyd aggressively exerted his waiver authority to

> grant Yeager his test pilot school diploma. It was only then that the famous Chuck Yeager officially became a test pilot.

There is something extra-enticing about elements of an innovation journey that yield incredible returns on investment. Those often come in the form of *non-material solutions*. That phrase, which essentially means there are ways to solve problems or discover solutions that do not require the creation of a novel thing or the purchase of a new item, is one we frequently use in the test and acquisition communities. It is a prime example of the truth that you can use your minds instead of your checkbooks to innovate. In the case of military aviation, non-material solutions could be new tactics, techniques, procedures, doctrine, education, organization, training, or policy that use the equipment we already have in a new way to meet requirements or yield unexpected operational advantages. After all, as I confidently stated in the Innovation Manifesto—the next war will be won by the best minds, not by the most might.

In a culture of innovation, these non-material solutions create huge wins. Because they don't require a large amount of resources to create something new, their returns can be staggering—a large gain with little cost. In our journey at The Center of the Aerospace Testing Universe, we had already explored these concepts through quick wins with notecard-ideas on the first day of my time as wing commander, deliberate process changes, and strategic delegations of authority. Yet, the non-material solution that resonated most with our workforce was the pursuit of waivers.

The fifth decision-making criteria described in Chapter 11 is: "What authorities are required to make a change" This is a key question to consider at every level of an organization in order to explore your own authorities and decide where you need relief from rules, policies or procedures from a higher level in the organization. These come in the form of waivers, and, at Edwards, we knew there were plenty of waivers that could streamline our procedures, eliminate barriers to our force, and demonstrate our commitment to creating an environment of trust

CHAPTER THIRTEEN ♣ NON-MATERIAL SOLUTIONS | 131

throughout the various levels of our team. So, we created a fun and competitive concept called the *Summer of Waivers*.

During this portion of our innovation journey, we were committed to aggressively considering waiver requests from our team. There were a few key elements of our Summer of Waiver pursuits essential to cultivating the trust of our team. First, the waivers had to make their way to me quickly for consideration—within a week of submission. No one in the chain of command could unnecessarily delay the process (in Congress, doing so would be called a pocket veto). We were watching and tracking. Second, no one between the person who submitted the waiver and me could reject it. They could recommend disapproval with sound rationale, but they could not stop it at their level. These ground rules would keep the waiver machine flowing, and I enjoyed the onslaught that made it to my desk.

Our wing front office team, led by Major Thomas "JIFKO" Stuart, Major Jonah "Rambo" Guadjardo, and Ms. Rebecca "Sis" Schweitzer, acted as juggernauts in the tracking and processing of these great waiver request ideas.

Of course, there were concerns with our waiver plans. In the middle of a meeting with the Hustle Squad about the concept, an officer on our team stood up and said, "We can't do this! It is challenging what it means to be in the Air Force. The Air Force's identity is about rules and regulations." Sadly, this officer thought that the Air Force wasn't about flying, fighting, or winning, rather about maintaining the status quo through rules and regulations. Such resistance was exactly what we were hoping to break through with the Summer of Waivers and, to some extent, through our entire innovation journey fueled by an unleashed workforce and the *listen, consider,* and *act* cycle.

In the end, the team submitted over a hundred waiver requests, and I only disapproved three of them. I was overwhelmingly happy with our Summer of Waivers campaign because we discovered and broke down dozens of barriers. The results provided a mechanism to slash those things that were hindering the mission and harming quality of life. Two popular successes pop to mind.

One example came from those working on the aircraft under the blazing high-desert sun asking for some relief from the normal uniform requirements of a military maintainer. Specifically, they wanted a waiver granting permission to wear shorts instead of pants or overalls while working. In my mind, it was an easy waiver to approve, especially because the entire maintenance chain of command supported doing so, and there was no accompanying downside. *Listening, considering,* and *acting* via a waiver in this situation was a big hit with our force.

Another example came from our active workforce with growing families. Those parents had childcare needs, and we had a full complement of on-base daycare and school facilities to handle these natural components of family life. Yet, whenever a military parent dropped off their kids, they had to put on their uniform hat. Imagine having to carry a baby in one arm with a diaper bag precariously hanging on your shoulder while dragging another child by the hand and putting on and taking off a hat while hoping that the strong desert wind doesn't carry it away with the rolling tumbleweeds. The waiver request was simple—eliminate the outdoor uniform hat requirements around these educational and childcare facilities. That waiver request, like the rest, got to me quickly, and we *listened, considered,* and *acted* by approving an easy but helpful idea. Military parents around the base rejoiced, and just recently, the entire Air Force adopted this same concept!

To a certain extent, I was a bit disappointed in the Summer of Waivers. I truly wanted the waiver process to knock down every possible barrier that still existed in our organization, and the fact that I only turned down three requests meant that our workforce was not asking for waivers as aggressively as they could have. I wanted them to swing for the fences and force me to make tough decisions about bold waiver requests.

Although it didn't reach its full potential, the Summer of Waivers was still a success that provided proof that we were finding every possible way to *listen, consider,* and *act*. We were relentlessly purging those things from our environment that took unnecessary time, cost extra money, and infringed on our quality of life or our pursuit of the mission.

CHAPTER THIRTEEN ♣ NON-MATERIAL SOLUTIONS | 133

We even followed up the Summer of Waivers with the Winter of Waivers to parlay our success from one to the other. We used the Boston Tea Party as our motivation for this event, when on December 16, 1773, a group of colonists boarded three British boats and dumped 342 boxes of tea into Boston harbor. It was a tangible sign of frustration with the prevailing way to doing business and a willingness to jettison the status quo when it got in the way. That is exactly what we were doing with our waivers. We were most motivated by written thoughts from John Adams the day after the Tea Party:

"This is the most magnificent Movement of all. There is a Dignity, a Majesty, a Sublimity, in this last Effort of the Patriots, that I greatly admire. The People should never rise, without doing something to be remembered—something notable and striking. This Destruction of the Tea is so bold, so daring, so firm, intrepid and inflexible, and it must have so important Consequences, and so lasting, that I can't but consider it as an Epocha in History."

Our waiver process was going to be a part of our magnificent innovation movement, remembered as notable and striking, bold and daring. The consequences of our innovative spirit were critical to our nation.

As expected, several waiver requests required an authority above my level to approve, and we dutifully pushed those waiver submissions up the chain of command while making the best arguments possible to support them. Many of these were approved as well, while allowing the higher headquarters to reconsider several rules and policies that affected the entire force. There were some waiver requests, however, that were just so good that it was worth me taking risk of approving them at my level even though I did not officially have the authority to do so.

Around the time of the Summer of Waivers, it became clear that our innovation journey had become our actual organizational and professional identity. We had crossed the threshold of transformation where our innovative behavior was being primarily and powerfully driven by newly ingrained values, norms, and assumptions that would be self-perpetuating as we moved forward. We wanted the right way to commemorate that important realization.

During the waiver process, Technical Sergeant Chad Hardesty recommended that everyone at Edwards be authorized to wear a newly created TEST patch on our uniforms. Sergeant Hardesty, a security forces expert, sought a way to create and cement a sense of togetherness and community throughout our workforce that would help define our innovation journey together. His simple patch design intended to accomplish that important goal.

Test Pilot School (TPS) graduates are authorized to wear their blue TPS patch for the rest of their careers. It is a reminder of that intense, year-long educational, training and flying experience where a student is literally given a flight manual the day prior and told that they would be flying that aircraft the next day. Be ready! The flying at TPS included aircraft as eclectic as World War II trainer aircraft, Soviet-era fighters, modern fighters, gliders, floatplanes, transports, and even the Goodyear Blimp. I flew 27 different types of aircraft during my TPS experience.

Yet, while TPS graduates made up a core of our organization, the vast majority of our population was comprised of experts in a variety of disciplines and specialties who were not TPS graduates. They all wore patches that reflected their unit affiliation but nothing that tied them to the overarching test mission of The Center of the Aerospace Testing Universe.

In reality, the entire base was involved in test and evaluation, somewhere in the planning, support, execution, data analysis, or reporting phases of activity. They needed a way to declare that important identity, especially now that we were all knit together in a bold cultural transformation that had become our true cultural commonality.

Thus, when I received the waiver request for everyone to wear the TEST patch, it was easy to approve. While I didn't technically have this official authority, it was such an obvious way to further reinforce and support our culture that it was worth the minor risk of a slap on my hand by my

CHAPTER THIRTEEN ♠ NON-MATERIAL SOLUTIONS | 135

superiors (which never came). After all, the entire workforce at Edwards was involved in the most important test—the test of ideas. While there were a few complaints outside our organization about our new TEST patch, the concept was a huge hit with our workforce and quickly caught on to other test organizations around the Air Force.

After over a year of bureaucratic processes and considerations, while the members of the test community were unofficially wearing the TEST patch, the Air Force formally approved the concept. Now the members of the Edwards community and others proudly wear the TEST patch legally without the need for support from a rogue commander. Yet, the impact transcended the test community. Sergeant Hardesty's concept was recognized as so simple and powerful that it became a trend throughout the Air Force to create community, and dozens of career fields now have their own approved patch to designate belongingness to a broader group.

In approving the TEST patch without the authority to do so, I clung to the famous thought from Chuck Yeager who only graduated from Test Pilot School because of a leader who was willing to aggressively exercise his waiver authority: "Rules are made for those unwilling to make up their own—but you better be right!" Fortunately, we were!

While taking risk with waiver authority can make sense at times, it is important to realize that the authority, resources, and influence are not always in the hands of a senior leader. Yet, this is not a threat nor a challenge but a golden opportunity. Just like using other people's money, finding ways to expand the team to pursue transformation and ignite impact can be a win-win for you and others. It is this element of non-material solutions that will be the focus on the next chapter.

ACTION ITEMS

Action Item 1: Take appropriate risks to further important transformational efforts.

Action Item 2: Intentionally focus efforts on community building to ingrain shared values, norms, assumptions, and identity.

Action Item 3: Break down barriers and ignite innovation through a period of widespread waiver activity in your organization.

CHAPTER FOURTEEN

SHARED HUMANITY AND MUTUAL BENEFIT

On May 2nd, 1776, the nations of Spain and France each committed the equivalent of a million dollars in weapons and ammunition to the American revolutionary cause. Such a commitment provided badly needed equipment to the Americans who had faced a tough year of fighting against the British. More importantly, this commitment encouraged and emboldened the colonists as well. Eight days later, riding the wave of support from their allies, the Second Continental Congress voted to allow the formation of independent colonial governments. This single act of bravery by the unified Continental Congress set the stage for subsequent acts of bravery. That resolution formally triggered a period of preparation for independence, laying the foundation for success. Two months later, the encouraged, emboldened American colonies signed the Declaration of Independence.

Life is not a solo sport; neither is leadership or innovation. We all need the equipping, encouraging, and emboldening that comes with strong, trusting relationships. All too often our rugged independence, a positive characteristic in many situations, causes us to neglect such relationships and try to solve our problems on our own.

In doing so, we lose an important force multiplier that comes with friendships, partnerships, and collaborations based on shared humanity and mutual benefit.

In an adversarial environment, especially in the political realm, it is easy to see life as a zero-sum game. If someone wins, that means someone equally loses. There is only a fixed portion of benefits and rewards, and everyone is a competitor. This outlook, much like the fixed mindset of Chapter 11, prompts stagnation and limitation. Finding ways for shared humanity and mutual benefit, much like a growth mindset, prompts advancement and acceleration. It is a way to turbocharge innovation and break down barriers.

FLASHFORWARD TO IRAQ (2020-2021)

The most powerful example of this idea of shared humanity and mutual benefit came from my 14-month deployment to Iraq. As described in Chapter 9, because of my position as America's Senior Defense Official and Defense Attaché, I represented our nation's military to the Iraqi government. In spite of the challenges of COVID-19 and severe security concerns, my position required me to leave our compound on a regular basis to meet with senior Iraqi leaders. Specifically, my calendar included a weekly meeting with the intimidating Iraqi Chief of Defense (CHOD), General Abdul Amir Yarallah.

Yarallah was a long-term, highly decorated member of the Iraqi Army. He was known as a stern leader, true warrior, and ruthless authoritarian. His bushy mustache rivals Tom Selleck's, adding to his rugged look and tough demeanor. More intimidating was his close affiliation with the Iranian aligned militia groups that hated the American presence in Iraq.

These militias launched mortars at American-controlled facilities, hurled rockets at the showcase Iraqi Air Force base to chase away American contractors supporting the Iraqi F-16 Fighting Falcon program, ran drugs, extorted businesses to raise militia funds, and carried out ruthless assassinations. As Yarallah took his position as the CHOD shortly after I arrived at my deployment, I knew my challenges in dealing with him could be significant.

I sat down with the key leaders of my team, which included my very experienced cultural advisor Adnan Alhamoudi, to figure out how to approach this problem. During that brainstorming session, we came to two primary conclusions.

First, we needed to find ways to connect with Yarallah at the personal, human level. One of the greatest ways to do so would be to highlight our shared experiences in the battle against ISIS. Iraqis and Americans had fought, bled and died together fighting this common threat to humanity for the last several years. He had been on the front lines of this conflict, and the more we could connect through this commonality, the better we could move past some of the natural animosity.

Second, we needed to find ways to explore common interests. After all, he wanted to succeed in his new position, and that meant improving the sustainable capabilities of his proud military force. In many ways, the United States wanted the Iraqi security forces to improve their sustained military capabilities as well. This overlap provided a wealth of commonality we could explore for mutual benefit.

In the end, we needed to be emotionally intelligent and strategically savvy to connect with Yarallah and work together as human beings. We needed to be savvy enough to strategically understand the overlap of interests where we could explore the fertile ground of mutual benefit. On our side, we also used the connection derived through emotional intelligence to pull his circle of objectives slightly closer to ours to increase the overlap.

As a result of this mindset, our sessions with Yarallah were productive and professional. There were certainly times of tension, most notably when Yarallah sternly reminded me that we had recently killed his best friend—militia leader Abu Mahdi al-Muhandis. Yet, we were able to work through these issues because we had a reason and connection to do so.

There are stakeholders all around us, and the vast majority don't have the level of innate hostility towards you or your cause as General Abdul Amir Yarallah had with us and ours. In fact, there are many stakeholders who enjoy significant overlap with you and your organization in their common objectives. In each of these cases, a bit of emotional intelligence and strategic savvy can allow you and your team to expand your efforts through win-win solutions that harness shared humanity and mutual benefit.

I previously learned the power of this concept in Washington, D.C. But, not to make a political statement in the midst of an apolitical leadership, innovation, and transformation book, if I was able to work productively and professionally with Yarallah, our political parties should be able to do the same even more so by working across the aisle. After all, there should be plenty of shared humanity and mutual benefit here in our environment that is not characterized by Iranian-supported rocket and mortar attacks, kidnappings and assassinations.

FLASHBACK TO JOINT BASE ANDREWS (2016-2018)

When I arrived as the commander of Joint Base Andrews, America's Airfield, I was excited and a bit nervous to get started. After all, there are a lot of eyes on a leader at a place like that, and I was not sure who would be on my side as an ally, advocate, and source of mutual support. Although previously, some had created an environment of selfishness, jealousy and division, I quickly discovered that one of the mission-partner wing commanders at Andrews and I were kindred spirits.

Colonel Casey Eaton was a world-class leader, and we committed to one another at our first meeting to selflessly work together towards achieving our mission and further the quality of life of our workforce and their families. We did so throughout our tenure, alongside of

CHAPTER FOURTEEN ♣ SHARED HUMANITY AND MUTUAL BENEFIT | 141

our Navy colleague Captain Scott "Sparkj" Fuller and others. It even meant that Sparkj and I would go toe-to-toe in front of our organizations (twice) in large sumo wrestling costumes and battle it out to bring honor to our teams and our services. Fortunately, the videos never went viral. But along the way, we became friends as we found plenty of shared humanity and mutual benefit.

While a military base seems a bit like an island, it isn't. This is especially true in the huge communities of Washington, D.C. and Prince George's County, Maryland. At Joint Base Andrews (JBA), we were an even match with the University of Maryland for the largest employer in the county, and our economic impact was over $2.2 billion annually. As a result, there were plenty of opportunities for engagement with local, county, state, and national leaders for mutual benefit. The first ally I met outside of the fence line of the base was my honorary commander, Mr. Jim Estepp.

Jim, a long-term resident and mainstay of the community, was the CEO of the Greater Prince George's Business Roundtable, a large business and community executive forum, and its subsidiary, the Andrews Business and Community Alliance, that focused on base relations. The honorary commander program could be a limited ceremonial endeavor, but I quickly learned from Jim that it could also be much more than that. This was a chance to highlight shared humanity and pursue mutual benefit.

Together, we did so with fervor, finding ways to collaborate within areas such as education, military spouse employment, housing, traffic patterns, garbage and recycling collection, support to food banks, emergency response, noise abatement, and safety mitigation. We even managed to pitch JBA as a potential location for the new FBI headquarters.

On April 5th, 2017, Captain Jonathan "Holster" Morgan took off from Joint Base Andrews in his F-16 and immediately experienced major engine problems, so he circled-back over the Potomac River and pointed his multi-million-dollar aircraft towards the base for an engine-out landing. At that point, in a subpar, expensive glider, he was over a heavily populated area with the increasing likelihood that he would have to eject. Doing his best to get back to base, he was constantly aware of the ground coming up quickly in his F-16 windscreen and needed to find the best place to point the aircraft to minimize the damage to the population on the ground.

At a height well below the recommended ejection altitude, Captain Morgan pulled the ejection handles. His carefully aimed F-16 slammed into a wooded area in the midst of a large neighborhood, harmlessly burning trees but nothing else. Around that time, Holster's parachute deployed from his ejection seat, and he swung for a couple of seconds under the silk canopy before finding himself safely on the ground.

Back at Andrews, a call had gone out to the leadership team that an F-16 was returning to base with a severe emergency. As the wing commander, I called for our Crisis Action Team (CAT), an emergency response cell, to form at our command post. I had led a CAT several times during emergency drills but never during a real emergency. It was time to learn quickly.

As we arrived at the command post in a room full of screens, telephones, computers, and radio systems, there was a lot of conflicting information about what had happened. Was the pilot alive or dead? Had the aircraft crashed into a school or a populated neighborhood as some reports had indicated? Was there a problem with our on-base aviation fuel system that could affect other aircraft, including Air Force One? Had jettisoned fuel tanks created an ecological disaster site near the Potomac River?

As we worked through the details of what happened, we had important roles in coordinating the pilot rescue, managing the emergency response, securing the off-base crash scene, working with local first responders, communicating with Air Force leadership, establishing a public affairs plan, and beginning the safety investigation. We marched through our processes, as we had in our emergency drills, with poise and professionalism, our heart rates spiking whenever updates filtered in.

CHAPTER FOURTEEN ♣ SHARED HUMANITY AND MUTUAL BENEFIT | 143

As expected, Air Force leadership thirsted for information from us, and we prioritized our efforts in the highly demanding situation the best we could. There were other, more local constituencies eager for information as well, but based on regulations, there were major limits about what we were allowed to share.

I harkened back to the nine months of my time in my position, thinking of my relationship with Jim and the lessons he taught me. I reflected upon how strong our bond had become with the community and what an important collaboration our relationship provided for mutual benefit. We could not properly achieve our mission and care for our workforce without these community partners. And now, they were rightfully interested in what was happening with our F-16 that was burning in *their* community.

So, when the time was right, with respect to my other responsibilities, I slightly disregarded protocol and stepped outside of the CAT to make some calls that were not on our response checklist. At that point, I briefly reached out to chat with community and state leaders, as well as the staff members of our Congressional delegation. I walked the line carefully to not overshare nor prompt unhelpful speculation, but I did provide them all the information they deserved to know in a sign of goodwill and partnership that punctuated our shared humanity and mutual interests.

This decision ranks as one of my most significant actions during my time in command of Andrews. It cemented a collaborative relationship, enshrined mutual respect and trust, and demonstrated the important truth that leadership best thrives through partnership. After that incident, our collaboration skyrocketed. When it was time for the Andrews air show in the fall of that year, the community went out of their way to provide extra support, especially in the form of a substantial contingent of community first responders who aided in support of our massive event.

Additionally, when it was time for Congress to finalize their authorization and appropriation for the military budget for the next year, I was personally asked to provide my top priorities by our Congressional delegation. As a result, two major construction projects were funded that would have otherwise not made it into the approval category. The children of our workforce would get a badly needed renovated childcare facility, and our large contingent of military working dogs would get a new and long-overdue kennel. It was an oversized impact that directly traced back to a few phone calls during an emergency situation.

Eight days later, when I arrived in the Mojave Desert to command Edwards Air Force Base, these lessons were still fresh in my mind. As a result, I knew that one of the lynchpins to our success on base would be thriving community relationships. After all, there are bountiful opportunities for shared humanity and mutual benefit everywhere.

On the Friday evening after my first week in command, the Edwards Air Force Base Civilian-Military Support Group (Civ-Mil Group, for short) hosted a large barbeque dinner at a ranch in the rugged desert mountains surrounding the Aerospace Valley. I was their guest of honor, and it was an ideal venue to get to know the community leaders who would be my primary partners for collaboration during my tenure. I immediately felt welcome as a part of this broader team and committed to put into good effect the lessons I learned so poignantly from Jim Estepp at Andrews.

Al Hoffman, Lisa Moulton and Bret Banks were my primary community collaborators. Congressman Steve Knight was also in attendance, and we immediately connected with one another. He was born at Edwards, son of the famous test pilot and fastest man in human history—X-15 pilot Pete Knight, who reached a record Mach 6.7 in 1967 as he screamed across the desert landscape in this revolutionary rocket plane. I also met a man named Art Thompson, who was perhaps the greatest innovative mind you have never heard of. He designed the B-2 bomber on the back of a napkin, while also creating the Batmobile, the world's largest paper airplane, and the Red Bull Stratos space capsule.

With people like this on my side, there were many rich opportunities for collaboration, innovation and partnership.

CHAPTER FOURTEEN ♣ SHARED HUMANITY AND MUTUAL BENEFIT | 145

As I talked to the Civ-Mil Group, it was clear they wanted to support whatever we were doing on base. They were even looking for a project they could adopt as their own. Airman Leadership School (ALS) is the course where each base trains its newest leaders, those young airmen who have risen to the ranks of being a first-level supervisor for other young airmen. We had a series of creative ALS Commandants who had a vision for making their campus a unique and welcoming learning environment, but they needed financial assistance to do so. This would be a perfect application of Other People's Money (OPM) that could help us implement innovative ideas as a springboard to raise our newest leaders.

The Civ-Mil Group was as thrilled to engage in this endeavor, and we were grateful for their investment. The ALS is now a thriving campus unlike any other in the Air Force. Additionally, there were other items we needed help with that were above the traditional Civ-Mil Group's capabilities, and their advocacy could help us reach the ones whose influence might be sufficient to move the needle on our efforts.

About a decade prior, the team at Edwards helped design and test a capability for the F-16 known at Automatic Ground Collision Avoidance System (Auto-GCAS), along with the Air Force Research Lab, NASA, and Lockheed-Martin. It was a novel capability that would automatically take over the flight control system the moment an aircraft was about ready to hit the ground. It would save the aircraft and its pilot during spatial disorientation or the temporary blackout that comes from maneuvering too aggressively.

Auto-GCAS had to be carefully designed to not takeover the aircraft too early and disrupt the intentional aggressive combat maneuvering of the pilot but never too late such that the pilot would be unable to avoid hitting the ground. The tolerance had to be extremely precise, and the team brilliantly figured out the right mechanism and algorithm to do so.

The Auto-GCAS system has been the safety net for a dozen saves where we would have otherwise lost a valuable aircraft and precious pilot in the burning wreckage of a horrible crash. I have watched several cockpit recorder videos that show Auto-GCAS saving the day, and they still bring a tear to my eye and goosebumps to my arms. This technology was an ingenious life-saving design from our predecessors at The Center of the Aerospace Testing Universe.

However, this system was also needed on the new F-35 aircraft to prevent loss of life and aircraft, but the program schedule didn't account for its installation until the middle of the 2020s. By then, the F-35 fleet worldwide would have suffered several tragic losses, which was unacceptable, especially when we knew that the Auto-GCAS system was mature, proven and successful. It was time to call in some favors from our broader community so we could innovate effectively.

Our large base is located in two Congressional Districts represented in 2018 by Congressmen Steve Knight and Kevin McCarthy. With the pull of a then-Majority Leader on our side, maybe we could nudge the programmatic planners to incorporate Auto-GCAS earlier than planned. It was a bold move to circumvent the chain of command, but a member of our team, Lt Col Tucker "Cinco" Hamilton, was passionately committed to this innovative move to support the warfighter as he walked into the Majority Leader's office to share his concerns alongside an accelerated proposal.

Cinco's arguments were successful, and the DoD was given Congressional direction to accelerate their plans. The team designed, tested, and fielded the F-35 Auto-GCAS thoroughly in record time. It is now a life-saving capability on this aircraft that has been proliferated throughout the United States Air Force, United States Navy, United States Marine Corps, and a growing list of allies and partners worldwide.

The Collier Trophy, a 500-pound award sitting in the National Air and Space Museum in Washington, D.C., is given each year "for the greatest achievement in aeronautics or astronautics in America." I have proudly been a part of two teams that won this lofty recognition. As a young test pilot, I was part of the team that won the 2006 Collier Trophy for the design and test of the F-22 Raptor. And because of the work of an amazing Auto-GCAS team, kickstarted by the bold and creative conversation initiated by Cinco and supported by Majority Leader McCarthy, the Edwards team was a key part of the 2018 award "for successfully completing a rapid design, integration, and flight test of critical, lifesaving technology for the worldwide F-35 fleet, expanding the technology for F-16 users and civil aviation, and setting certification standards that marked aviation's entry into the age of autonomy." This is a true example of innovative collaboration through shared humanity and mutual benefit.

While it is tough to match the mission-related impact of Auto-GCAS, there was a quality-of-life related item that could generate equal impact for military families—solving challenges with military spouse employment. As Dragon's Lair inputs echoed the feedback from military spouses on base, and as the Spouse Hustle Squad initiated their innovative activity focused on solving family-related issues, there was an overwhelming trend. A top concern of our population was related to unemployment and underemployment of military spouses.

As of this writing, military spouses are unemployed at a rate that is six times greater than the national unemployment average, and underemployment is even worse. Part of the problem is military deployments regularly create single-parent families with unique childcare concerns. An additional part of the problem is the instability of frequent military moves that uproot a spouse and hinder career continuity. Yet, the biggest part of the problem seemed to be the lack of portability of military spouse licenses and certifications.

When a military spouse moves from one state to another, their license does not automatically travel with the spouse. While they were fully qualified to work in one state—as a doctor, teacher, nurse, hairdresser, lawyer, etc.—they are no longer officially qualified when they move to another state. I've talked to spouses that had to spend a year of extra training and over $8,000 in training fees just to requalify in a new state even though the skills they brought with them met the same standards. This single item creates major problems with recruiting and retention of military personnel while robbing communities of highly professional workers that could fill employment gaps immediately if the rules were different. This was more than an Edwards problem; it was a national problem.

I started my lobbying efforts by first speaking to California state leaders about the value of automatically accepting licenses from newly arrived military spouses, similar to a ground-breaking program implemented in Utah. I walked around the statehouse sharing my concerns and ideas and, while there were many sympathetic legislators, they seemed to be hindered by the powerful professional interest groups that protected in-state jobs through onerous certification processes. We made a bit of progress in that way, but nothing that would ultimately resolve the issue. Amid my zealous advocacy for our military families, however, I captured the attention of Congressional candidate Mike Garcia.

Mike was a previous Navy fighter pilot who was extra sensitive to my well-reasoned argument about the need for spouse license portability and reciprocity during military moves from one state to another. He was running for the Congressional seat previously held by Steve Knight and was seemingly committed to solving this issue through federal legislation.

After he won the election, he tackled a variety of issues that demanded his attention, but he never forgot about the importance of military spouse employment. Though it was long after I left Edwards, I was beaming with pride when President Joe Biden signed legislation in December of 2022, authored and argued by Congressman Mike Garcia, that required states to accept the licenses of our military spouses as they moved around the country.

It was a huge boost to 132,000 military spouses in licensed career fields, and it all started with a series of good ideas from Edwards that were listened to, considered, and *acted* upon through a partnership of shared humanity and mutual benefit. To us at Edwards, the support of these relationships was like a million-dollar boost from the countries of Spain and France to the fledgling American revolutionary cause.

ACTION ITEMS

Action Item 1: Utilize emotional intelligence and strategic savvy! It will allow you and your team to expand your efforts through win-win solutions that harness shared humanity and mutual benefit.

Action Item 2: Aggressively seek expanded partnerships that allow for collaboration and innovation.

CHAPTER FIFTEEN

YOUR GREATEST IDEA

On June 3rd, 1980, unbeknownst to the vast majority of humanity, the world faced a nuclear catastrophe that nearly ended humankind as we know it. In the midst of especially high tensions with the Soviet Union, the early warning screens at NORAD detected 2 inbound Soviet missiles. A few moments later, 220 missiles were detected, and that number increased to over 2,000 shortly thereafter. As split-second decisions were passed up the chain of command on how to respond, nuclear alert crews scrambled to their bombers, and launch messages were prepared for the missile fields and submarine captains, the missiles on the screens disappeared without a trace. No missiles struck our nation. The same scenario happened three days later.

Maintenance troubleshooting crews rushed to determine the cause of the false alarm. They quickly converged upon the culprit—the failure of a single, 46-cent computer chip. When that chip failed, it transmitted a 2 instead of a 0. In the computer code, that numerical value was translated into the number of inbound missiles, increasing in order of magnitude each time the signal was sent through the complicated early warning system. Senior military leaders and their technical experts were reminded of an important fact—every part matters and nothing in the system should be discounted, minimized, or marginalized.

As leaders of an innovation journey and organizational transformation, this lesson applies to us as well. Every part matters, each step forward is important, and nothing in your journey should be discounted, minimized, or marginalized. The smallest element of movement is a part of your entire portfolio of progress, and the sum total of the tiniest successes can provide magnificent momentum.

At my final Commander's Call before giving up command at The Center of the Aerospace Testing Universe, I was asked a great question by an anonymous audience member—*"Of all the innovation activity and progress that occurred during your tenure, what was the best idea of them all?"*

It is important to note that we were in the midst of Dragon Bingo when this question arrived. Every member of the audience had a bingo chart populated with some of my most-used phrases and terms. Whoever completed a bingo line first would stand up in the huge auditorium and yell "Bingo!" and be rewarded from an awesome tray of baked treats by my wonderful wife. Thus, it is possible that the question was just a ruse to prompt me to utter a phrase that would help the person asking the question complete their bingo sheet, but I'm choosing to chalk it up to a great question because I am an eternal optimist.

As I considered the question, a tidal wave of ideas crashed through the forefront of my mind. There were big ideas, good ideas, some successful and some not. There were mission-related, family-initiated, quality of life, and mission-support ideas. There were 46-cent ideas and hundred-dollar ideas. Yet, my answer to the large crowd on that day was easy. *"The best idea was to listen to all of your ideas."*

The sum of their ideas massively changed the culture of our base, and the results were revolutionary. Our cultural change was triggered by the *listen, consider,* and *act* cycle, and it all started with a willingness to *listen*. Our success was catalyzed by a culture that embraced a powerful concept of humility, approachability, and credibility—a close cousin to the previously-addressed concept of wisdom and humility.

CHAPTER FIFTEEN ♣ YOUR GREATEST IDEA

The United States Air Force Weapons School is the Air Force equivalent of the Navy's Top Gun. The graduates from this grueling six-month course complete their training at a location that is a three-hour drive through the Mojave Desert from Edwards to a place known as Nellis Air Force Base. It sits on the outskirts of Las Vegas, Nevada and produces tactical experts and warfighting leaders. They are tasked with being superb at their warfighting craft and expected to replicate themselves by producing a squadron full of tactical experts. It is through this process that the USAF maintains its decided edge, producing absolute air dominance for the last seventy years.

The Weapons School creates these warrior mentors and leaders by expecting them to embody three critical characteristics—being Humble, Approachable, and Credible. The last of the three is likely the easiest for a graduate as they permanently wear a grey graduate patch characterized by its predominant bullseye on their left shoulder, indicating their ability to withstand the rigors of the school's demanding syllabus. Yet, without the first two characteristics, these tactical experts would never be able to replicate themselves. They would likely survive any engagement due to their individual prowess, but their supporting force would crumble around them, and the enemy would win the battle. Thus, they are reminded by their instructor cadre that humility and approachability are as important as credibility. If they weren't humble, then they would stop learning. If they weren't approachable, then no one would learn from them. Without all three, the Air Force Weapons School could never produce a complete fighting force that maximizes its impact and ensures our nation's future.

Leaders in all venues and at all levels must embrace this important truth and these three critical characteristics. We need to embody them in our classrooms, boardrooms, and courtrooms. We need them to attract others to our ideas, fields, and professions. We need them to properly mentor, instruct, explain, and influence. We need them to stay current and relevant. We need them to remain related and interconnected to the broader world around us. While we must continue to applaud credibility, we must equally uplift humility and approachability to maximize our impact and secure our future.

There is an interesting corollary to Humble, Approachable, and Credible—the Dunning-Kruger Effect. It is explained in a 1999 academic publication in the *Journal of Personality and Social Psychology* entitled "Unskilled and Unaware of It: How Difficulties in Recognizing One's Own Incompetence Lead to Inflated Self-Assessments." It's a classic! The authors, David Dunning and Justin Kruger, statistically and methodically demonstrate that people with the lowest competence or skill in a particular area have the worst ability to judge their own competence or skill, which often massively inflates their perception of both. On the flip side, those with the highest competence or skill in a particular area tend to underestimate it.

These findings should blast warning signals to all of us. If we think we are skilled or competent, then buyer beware, we may actually be unskilled and incompetent. If we think we are lacking, then we are actually less likely to be so. This duality harkens back to the moment when my wife was declared ready to defend her dissertation in a grueling chemistry PhD program at the University of California at Berkley. At a point of exhaustion from the overwhelming nature of it all, she acknowledged that she felt like she knew nothing. It was that intellectual trigger of humility and approachability that proved her credibility. Based on that admission, she was prepared to defend her brilliant dissertation and graduate!

The listen, consider, and *act* cycle is the manifestation of a humble, approachable and credible culture. It is also the antidote to the Dunning-Kruger effect. It opens the organization to the power of collective intelligence that overcomes individual limitations. It was the core of our innovation journey at Edwards and proof that a bunch of 46-cent wins can be massive.

Every idea in Dragon's Lair, every concept on the day-one notecards, every receptive conversation, every idea submitted during our innovation campaigns, and every waiver had added up to something that was powerful. Even the simplest of ideas yielded oversized results in our large-scale idea-generation machine. All of this was activated by humility, approachability, and credibility.

CHAPTER FIFTEEN ♣ YOUR GREATEST IDEA

When you keep your ears open, through humility and approachability, you never know what you will learn or how you can add to your credibility. One of the ideas that came in through our various solicitations was to create an indoor playground on base. To me, a guy with kids that were older than the population that cares about playgrounds, this seemed like a small idea without much impact. After all, we had several outdoor playgrounds scattered around the housing areas of our base. As we asked around, however, it became apparent that this was an idea with a massive following.

In the high desert it is almost always windy and typically unpleasant to linger outside. While kids don't usually mind such inconveniences, the adults who supervise them do. Add in the blistering temperatures in the summertime, and it makes an indoor playground option very attractive. The question, then, was where to build it.

There are a lot of buildings on a base the size of Edwards, but most of the space is either accounted for or not suitable for a playground facility. We couldn't build a stand-alone facility for such a recreational activity, or it would break the bank. As a result, we squinted with our ears (a great phrase used by the former Chief of Staff of the Air Force, General David Goldfein) and found a brilliant option.

We were fortunate to have a large bowling alley on base, and while it was popular, it was extremely rare to have every lane full. Why couldn't we repurpose two bowling lanes and turn them into our indoor playground? The result would be a bowling alley that would become a multi-purpose recreational facility, with plenty of bowling lanes remaining and a space for the kids to play indoors.

Business in the bowling alley would likely increase because of the flow of additional customers taking advantage of the food and drink service provided while they bowled or watched their children play. We did our research, and everything about the idea was positive and favorable. It was a win-win-win concept, and the families were thrilled. The simple idea paid huge dividends for the well-being of our community, and it was all because we had the humility and approachability to listen.

Speaking of kids, we had a booming on-base population and school system that was suitable to meet those needs. Living on base is a bit of a slice of old-fashioned America, allowing kids to walk or ride their bikes to school without the safety concerns requiring a parent escort in most of our modern-day society. Yet, one of the primary routes to school took the kids across one of the busiest roads on base. While there were properly placed Stop signs to shape the traffic flow, sometimes drivers would miss them, resulting in a few close calls. To this, a parent offered a simple solution, and we were *listening*.

One thing we didn't lack in the desert (in addition to wind) was sunshine. The parent's idea was to install a small patch of solar cells on the top of key Stop signs to power flashing red LED lights around the perimeter of the sign. Our research revealed that it would cost almost nothing to make these changes while reinforcing the existence and importance of those Stop signs along the primary routes traveled by the students.

With the purchase of material almost as simple as a 46-cent chip in a missile warning computer system, we provided added protection to our kids as they blissfully traveled to school. The implementation of every idea was not always as simple, but each started with a dose of humility and approachability to activate the *listen, consider,* and *act* cycle.

When I think of Humble, Approachable, and Credible, the names and faces of several leaders flash through my mind. The successful performance of their organizations bears record to the power of this key concept. There is no leader, however, who better typifies these essential characteristics than now-retired Colonel Ryan "Cujo" Blake. Cujo was a graduate from both the University of Texas and Stanford University, a highly decorated F-15E combat pilot, and an immensely well-respected leader in the flight test community. As credible as he was in every respect, he was also humble and approachable.

I had heard of Cujo throughout my career but never had the opportunity to work directly with him prior to my assignment at Edwards. During my time as the commander there, Cujo was the Commandant of the famed United States Air Force Test Pilot School, and it was a joy to see him in action every single day. He had a powerful commitment and genuine care and concern for our community, his people and his team. In doing so, he *listened,* he *considered,* and he *acted.*

An idea that had been batted about for a while in the test community was creating a Space Test Pilot School for the military's space systems. While the idea sounds a bit fanciful, the main job of a test pilot or a flight test engineer is to be the recognized expert in test and evaluation. Thus, these space test professionals would not necessarily be flying anything in the traditional sense but would ensure the test and evaluation activities for all space systems would deliver capabilities that best met warfighter requirements.

After settling into his Commandant position, Cujo immediately started *listening* to his team as they expressed a firm interest in bringing this concept to life. He unleashed his experts while guiding the process using his bold vision and supportive demeanor. He also spoke up about the broad benefits of such a course and found allies in the space, test, and acquisition communities. As he *listened, considered,* and *acted,* his team came up with a brilliant plan that created a concept that would add massive value to the warfighter in the space domain. As a result of those efforts, the Space Test Course is now a regular fixture at TPS.

Its graduates are literally shaping every space system in the Space Force's arsenal to provide space dominance in ways that would have never taken place without the humble, approachable, and credible leadership style of Cujo Blake. And just like the very successful leaders of his ilk, Cujo would eagerly tell you that his greatest idea was *listening* to the ideas of his team, even when they initially seemed like 46-cent parts.

ACTION ITEMS

Action Item 1: Always remember that every part matters and no one and no idea in your organization should be discounted, minimalized, or marginalized.

Action Item 2: Embrace the important concept that each step forward is important. The smallest element of movement is a part of your entire portfolio of progress, and the sum total of the tiniest successes can provide magnificent momentum.

Action Item 3: Carefully listen to the ideas of your team—it will be your best leadership idea.

Action Item 4: Embrace the key characteristics of humility, approachably, and credibility. These traits catalyze the *listen, consider,* and *act cycle.*

CHAPTER SIXTEEN

DARING WINS!

Test pilot, inventor, and innovator Wilbur Wright warned about the challenges of pursuing powered flight when he said that "the man who wishes to keep at the problem long enough to really learn anything positively must not take dangerous risks. Carelessness and overconfidence are usually more dangerous than deliberately accepted risks." In this statement, Wright explicitly warns against taking dangerous risks. Yet, there is an implied nugget of wisdom in this quote that the innovative minded among us must not neglect. Wright suggests that positive progress requires professionals to take carefully considered and deliberately accepted risks. Wilbur Wright never says to avoid *all* risk, only to avoid *unsound* risk.

French visionary Louis Pierre Mouillard wrote the brilliant work L'Empire de l'Air in 1881. This test pilot, aviation pioneer, and early aviation hero boldly tackled his passion for aviation as both a fanciful artist and cutting-edge inventor. Mouillard's aviation intellect was decades ahead of its time, and his writing, thinking, and drawing provided powerful inspiration to aviation pioneers like the Wright Brothers.

In his closing paragraph, Mouillard wrote the following: "Finally, I counsel the greatest possible prudence to all who undertake to solve the problem of sailing flight. Let them carefully canvass all the causes of accidents which it is possible to foresee; but once they have made this canvass, once they have completed their researches, I recommend them to act with energy and will, and I know of no better word to say to them than the one with which I began this monograph: 'Osez'—Daring Wins!"

Like Wilbur Wright, Mouillard recommends that those pursuing aviation milestones should embrace the greatest reasonable prudence. Aviation pioneers are to be cautious, not reckless. But, more explicitly than Wilbur, Mouillard goes on to promote an informed and bold measure of risk-taking to promote progress. He tells test pilots throughout the ages to adequately assess and mitigate risk then be bold in their pursuits. For Mouillard, test pilots, and leaders of innovation, a two-word phrase sufficiently captures the characteristic that properly promotes progress—Daring Wins!

An aircraft's envelope defines its approved and tested operating limits, primarily its top speed, maximum altitude, and most extreme maneuvering capabilities. Interestingly, a pilot operates at an aircraft's best performance at the edge of the envelope, just inside the maximum limits. There is a risk in operating so close to the boundaries, but the ideal performance exists in that regime. If you don't go far enough, you fail to max perform your aircraft. If you go too far, you will break it.

In Chapter 8, I briefly described the concept and power of paradigms. In *The Structure of Scientific Revolutions*, Thomas Kuhn argues that a crisis is a necessary condition for an organization to shake itself out of the paradigm. That fatalistic view dooms us all to failure and catastrophe when our assumptions, worldviews, or paradigms are wrong. According to Kuhn, we can neither assess nor mitigate risk because of the powerful blinders that accompany our paradigms. Yet, even pessimistic Thomas Kuhn provides an escape clause in his fine print.

Kuhn claims the rookie members of our team are "so young or so new to the crisis-ridden field that practice has committed them less deeply than most of their contemporaries to the world view and rules determined by the old paradigm." Essentially, Kuhn is saying that the newer and

CHAPTER SIXTEEN ♣ **DARING WINS!** | 161

younger members of our team are not yet trapped in the prevailing paradigm, and thus, are the only ones who can snap our organization out of a paradigm-induced danger before it is too late.

In essence, he is arguing for the power of the *listen, consider,* and *act* cycle that harnesses the fresh perspective of the younger members of a team who can shake an organization out of a paradigm before catastrophe strikes. It is their untarnished perspective about shortcomings, risks, and inadequacies that can make all the difference in avoiding crises and embracing progress as we boldly pursue innovative ideas and seek organizational change. The older members of the team are simply too stuck in their ways to adequately assess, mitigate, and accept risk, or execute boldly. The younger members can be the heroes that circumvent and preempt the crisis.

Every year, major commands in the United States Air Force bring their wing commanders and other senior leaders for a high-level leadership conference. The four-star general in charge of that major command hosts the event, and it provides an opportunity to understand their command philosophy, priorities, and intent. It's also a venue for dialogue across the organization to learn from one another and harness the best ideas of one's peers. I had the opportunity to attend these conferences while commanding Edwards, and I used the time to proudly share the details of our innovation journey to encourage other senior leaders to pursue something similar in their own organizations. After all, their workforces wanted to be unleashed too.

As a part of this event, I gave our four-star commander, General Arnie Bunch, a gift during my presentation about innovation. It wasn't pandering nor was it kissing up. It also wasn't an ordinary gift, rather a strategic statement about our innovation movement and the possibilities of an unleashed command climate characterized by the *listen, consider,* and *act* cycle. The gift was a copy of my favorite Culture Wall tile—"Find out where 'no' lives and kill it!" and what he did with this 12- by 12-inch display was brilliant!

At an appropriate time in the meeting, General Bunch invited the attendees to make a commitment to a command philosophy of rooting out the natural tendency of avoiding change while blindly embracing the status quo. Specifically, he offered the opportunity to sign the Culture Wall tile as a pledge to that commitment. Almost every attendee did so, and General Bunch hung the tile on his office wall as a source of motivation and a powerful reminder to fulfill that commitment.

The symbolism of that tile and those signatures was important for the people in the room and at the conference. Some leaders signed it because they actually believed in the commitment, and some likely did so because they were pressured into it. Most importantly, the word spread throughout the expansive major command about the tile and the leaders' signatures, potentially reaching a younger member of an organization run by one of the leaders in that room and empowering them to speak up when they would otherwise be too hesitant. Their thoughts may preempt the next crisis. Additionally, their ideas may launch a wider *listen, consider,* and *act* cycle that could improve risk management processes while simultaneously spurring a culture of boldness and a commitment to progress.

The test and evaluation profession is largely about risk management, and there is no progress to be made by avoiding risk. In order to succeed and survive, test pilots need to know, manage, and accept the risk. Specifically, a test pilot and their test team should consider three primary elements of their risk environment:

- What are the areas of risk?

- How does the team best mitigate those areas of risk?

- Who is the right approval authority to accept the remaining, unmitigated risk?

Once the team carefully assesses these things, they can execute a test with cautious but bold professionalism.

FLASHFORWARD TO IRAQ (2020-2021)

I had executed plenty of flight tests using this three-phase risk methodology during my three assignments at Edwards. Some were considered low risk, some medium, and some were considered high risk. But, shortly after arriving in Baghdad, I realized that I had the chance to use this test methodology and risk management rubric during my time in Iraq as well. This time it would be on the ground in a highly charged political environment that could be considered extreme risk.

The Iranian-aligned militia groups had been bold about launching rockets and mortars at the U.S. Embassy. Before the rockets would strike their targets, we would have a few seconds of warning that enabled us to quickly find protective cover. Otherwise, we were defenseless. Yet, there was an available option to provide a more active defense, one that had never been used at an embassy before. It was called the C-RAM.

Counter-Rocket, Artillery, Mortar (C-RAM) is a widely used system by the United States military that detects and tracks inbound projectiles with its acquisition and targeting system, then destroys or deflects these threats with a large-caliber machine gun. It literally shoots down rockets with bullets. Senior Department of State and Defense officials had concluded that we needed such a system to protect our otherwise vulnerable population, and it was up to our extended team to transport the system to the embassy and to make it operational. There were two big challenges in doing so.

The first obstacle was getting the components of this multi-gun system to the embassy. Hostile militia groups controlled many of the vehicle checkpoints in and around Baghdad, especially those along the route between Baghdad International Airport and the embassy near the center of the city. Our operational security needed to be tightly controlled so that these rogue and malign elements wouldn't know what we were doing. They would love to disrupt our plans and hijack our caravan of components. How we were able to do so is a miraculous feat of innovation and risk management on its own, but it goes beyond the scope of what is wise to put in print.

The second hurdle was qualifying the system as operational, and it was far more complicated than simply setting up the C-RAM as it had been designed. The system needed to be calibrated, which meant firing each of the guns to ensure that they would shoot their high speed 20-mm bullets at exactly the right location and distance as directed by the targeting system to effectively accomplish their defensive mission. We needed to perform this calibration in a contentious political environment where international relationships were already fraught with tension and violence. We also needed to do so safely in the middle of a major metropolitan area. C-RAM systems were typically designed to protect ships at sea or safeguard remote locations where collateral damage was not a factor. In a sprawling and densely packed capital city, inadvertent damage was a major concern.

We assembled a cross-functional team, including savvy diplomats, smart security experts, trusted cultural advisors, and experienced C-RAM professionals to thoroughly discuss the elements of risk with our calibration plans. We adjusted the dates, times, directions for fire, elevations of aim, and self-detonation characteristics of the bullets to reduce risk. This was an especially important planning effort to prevent our ammunition from striking something in the air or on the ground that would cause unwanted damage, sparking an international incident.

Next, we created a plan to mitigate as much of the remaining risk as possible, including clearing procedures, public affairs plans, contingency efforts, exercises regimes, and embassy internal announcements. The plan was so carefully considered that it reduced and mitigated risk to an amazingly small magnitude. Yet, we still needed to complete the final risk-related step, which was to get approval from the Ambassador to perform the calibration activities. As we did so, we had one specific element of remaining risk mitigation that needed his acknowledgment and approval.

CHAPTER SIXTEEN ♣ **DARING WINS!** | 165

There was a substantial political and international relations risk with the C-RAM plans that required high-level communication with senior Iraqi leaders. We determined that our relationship with the new Iraqi Prime Minister, Mustafa Al-Kadhimi, necessitated that we must not surprise him with our machine gun fire over his capital city. The best way to communicate to him about our calibration plans was via his military leadership, and the military leaders that would provide the most direct pathway to the Prime Minister were his Personal Secretary and his JOC-I Commander.

Prime Minister Kadhimi's Personal Secretary, General Mohammed Hamed Al Bayati, was a regular contact of mine during my time in Iraq. We typically met twice a month, and it provided a high-level access point directly to the Prime Minister for military matters. As a part of our mitigation, I shared details of our upcoming C-RAM activity with him at a neutral outdoor location so the prying ears that secretly listened to our normal indoor meetings could not catch our conversation.

General Hamed understood our need for such a defensive system that ultimately protected Iraq from a heavy-handed U.S. reaction to an American casualty from a militia rocket attack. He was very interested in the risk details as related to the Baghdad population, so that he could inform the Prime Minister of the risk and our mitigation activities. I left that meeting feeling good about his reception, especially because we made it clear that we were informing him, not asking for permission for our C-RAM calibration operations that had already been deemed essential.

The Joint Operations Command for Iraq (JOC-I) is the operational command structure for the Iraqi security apparatus, much like a Combatant Command in the United States. The JOC-I was led by General Abd al-Amir al-Shimmari, and he needed to understand the operational implications of our intense gunfire over Baghdad. A day before our planned C-RAM calibration test, I went to speak to him with my brilliant chief attaché and long-term foreign area officer, Colonel Elliot "El Jefe" Harris. The short timeline would best prevent a leak of our plans to the militias, while still giving the Iraqi military a sufficient time to prepare for our operations. It would also ensure that the Prime Minister would be doubly aware of our activities.

As expected, General al-Shimmari asked a lot of questions about risk management but was satisfied with our answers. If it hadn't been for El Jefe spilling hot tea on his own lap as it was served to him and jumping up and down as the liquid burned his crotch at the most sensitive part of my notification, everything would have been perfect. We walked away from that meeting convinced that we had received implied consent from the leadership of the JOC-I for our calibration plans.

The evening before our test, I received a series of calls through my amazing cultural advisor Adnan. The Prime Minister wanted to fully understand the C-RAM activities we were ready to perform, and with his Personal Secretary as our mediator, I went through each detail of our plan that was prudent to share. There was a period during that conversation where I thought Prime Minister Kadhimi was going to strongly object to our operations and try to stop them. As we explained our risk minimizing plan and our added mitigation efforts, however, he was satisfied. Thus, the calibration was a go for the next day.

As it turned out, the ideal day for the C-RAM test was the 4th of July. As the mid-day temperatures exceeded 115 degrees and the vast majority of Iraqis were spending the afternoon indoors to avoid the heat of the day, we sprayed streams of self-detonating bullets over Baghdad. After a few repeat fires to optimize calibration, we ceased our activities and called the C-RAM system fully operational. Other than a buzz of media activity, and the typical Iranian-fueled anti-American hate that didn't appreciate our Independence Day C-RAM activities, there were no injuries and no confirmed damage.

On the night of the 4th of July, the militia groups initiated their own fireworks by attacking the embassy. This time, their barrage of rockets was successfully engaged and countered by our new friend the C-RAM. Not only did our risk efforts pay off, but the embassy enjoyed a layer of defense previously absent.

> During every rocket attack after that, I would quickly duck and cover and wait for the loud firing of the steady stream of bullets from the C-RAM. Whenever I heard that distinct buzz, it brought a smile to my face and pride to my heart. Our risk management efforts had been successful as applied to this life-or-death situation.

These same risk management steps applied to a C-RAM calibration in Baghdad apply to leadership and innovation; assess, mitigate, accept risk, then be bold in your pursuits. If you are not willing to take a risk, you will not make progress. If you don't go far enough, you won't max perform your organization. If you go too far, you risk breaking everything. Assess, mitigate, accept, and execute. It takes courage and a willingness to go to the edge of the envelope to make true advancements. A leader must acknowledge that there is risk in promoting progress—personal risk, career risk, and reputational risk. But, without accepting this risk, a leader will be part of the countless masses of others who have accepted stagnation in order to embrace safety. Leaders are like pilots as described by Chuck Yeager: "An arrogant pilot will get ya killed; confident ones make history."

When you travel on a commercial airplane, occasionally a flight attendant will get on the intercom to tell the passengers that safety is their top priority. That is not true! Their top priority is actually getting paying customers to their destination on time with reasonable risk. If they wanted to eliminate risk, then they should stay on the ground.

When you take a trip to Disneyland or any other theme park, a ride attendant may say that safety is their number one priority. That is not true! Their top priority is providing the best overall entertainment and thrill to their guests at a reasonable risk. If they wanted safety to be the absolute priority, then they should shut down their rides and close the park. In reality, they have assessed, mitigated, and approved a reasonable risk, and are executing boldly.

I recently came across a powerful quote by British political philosopher John Stuart Mill that speaks to satisfaction and safety, happiness and humanity, risk and reward. Mill said, "Those only are happy who have their minds fixed on some object other than their own happiness; on the happiness of others, on the improvement of mankind, even on some art or pursuit, followed not as a means, but as itself an ideal end. Aiming thus at something else, they find happiness by the way."

If we truly desire to maximize our own happiness, then we should seek something that embodies a broader meaning and significance. Happiness and success are the byproduct of a life that pursues purpose outside of the alluring safety of stagnation. We can only thrive, innovate, and transform when we set elements of safety aside and take some risk. Daring Wins!

ACTION ITEMS

Action Item 1: Demonstrate moral courage and wise risk management in order to make positive and meaningful progress.

Action Item 2: Utilize the *listen, consider,* and *act* cycle to harness the fresh perspective of the younger members of a team who can shake an organization out of a paradigm before catastrophe strikes.

Action Item 3: Take the following steps to create a wise risk management culture:

- Determine the areas of risk.
- Make plans to best mitigate those areas of risk.
- Seek the proper approval authority to accept the remaining, unmitigated risk.
- Execute boldly; Daring Wins!

CHAPTER SEVENTEEN

CONTINUING ADVANTAGE

On a cool, crisp morning in February of 2020, I gave up command of Edwards Air Force Base. In the same hangar where I took command 19-months prior, I looked out over the large crowd assembled and reminisced about the incredible innovation journey we had taken together. I was awash with fond memories of this whirlwind assignment. With another F-22 as a backdrop and a stage dominated by a massive American flag hanging from the hangar ceiling, I gave my final remarks. I reminded those who were there on that beautiful desert morning that "this team has dwarfed the innovation activity for the rest of the United States Air Force" while setting the pace as the "benchmark wing-level organization for innovative activity."

I verbally reflected on our advantages at Edwards—amazing airspace, an amazing airfield, amazing acreage, and amazing aircraft. "But," I reminded our team, "our true national treasure are our amazing Airmen, and their families, and our mission partners, and our community partners." I closed with the thoughts, "You are a national treasure, and you are The Center of the Aerospace Testing Universe." I then walked back to my seat and set my mind on the challenges that I would face in the coming months as our nation's Senior Defense Official and Defense Attaché to a very hostile and unstable situation in Iraq. I even had scheduled pre-deployment activities that very afternoon.

My work at Edwards, though, was not yet complete. While I was no longer commander of that organization, our legacy would be judged by how it lived on into an uncertain future. As I walked off the stage, we were still innovating at an unprecedented pace, and the morale of the workforce was booming as a result of an environment of unleashed activity. In reality, it would be the next several months and years that would determine if we truly transformed the culture of our organization in the rugged and desolate Mojave Desert. To some extent, that story is still playing out as this story ends.

I once had an eccentric strategy professor, Dr Everett Dolman, with a unique definition of strategy. Most strategy definitions revolve around the confluence of *ends, ways,* and *means,* or more specifically, how *ways* and *means* produce *ends.* Dolman objected to such thinking because the word *ends* implies a strategy that has a finishing point. In reality, the *end* of one phase of a strategy is simply the initial condition of the next phase. Thus, Dr. Dolman's definition of strategy reinforces the long-term and sustainable nature of properly considered strategic activity—"a plan for continuing advantage."

Dolman's definition is a brilliant one for properly considered leadership as well—"a plan for continuing advantage." After all, success during a leader's tenure that falls apart after their departure is not success. At the end of one person's position as a leader, they should have created a well-positioned initial condition for long-term and sustainable success that enables a continuing advantage. That is the real metric of leadership success and a proper model to consider for the true vitality of an innovative journey.

As I was preparing for my deployment to Iraq in Washington, D.C., I heard talk of an anonymous, formal complaint about the use of funds during my tenure to create a makerspace that could be used by the entire base population, including the on-base schools, children, and spouses. It was one of those make-or-break moments that could have derailed the entire culture and thrown a wet blanket on the fires of innovation that had been burning bright at The Center of the Aerospace Testing Universe. Was there a message in this misfortune?

The COVID pandemic struck shortly thereafter, and the team at Edwards regrouped to deal with a new threat that was far more important than

CHAPTER SEVENTEEN ♣ CONTINUING ADVANTAGE | 171

a petty and unfounded complaint about a misuse of resources. Some members of the team, led in part by Chief Ian Eishen, saw an opportunity provided by the makerspace. They leapt into action, designing, prototyping and producing masks for the base population. Not only did their product meet the needs of those at Edwards, but their mask design became the standard for the entire United States Air Force. That single pivot during the most challenging of times cemented an extension of the innovation journey from one commander to the next, proving that the culture was alive and well, unbroken by a pandemic that followed closely on the heels of a leadership transition.

The Hustle Squad, renamed SparkED, continues to be the foundational bedrock and driving engine for an innovation culture that bubbles from the bottom up at Edwards. They have a new mascot but the same passion for the *listen, consider,* and *act* cycle. Through creative innovation campaigns, they have shepherded new projects, like Lime Scooters for the base population and a civilian leadership school to better develop the Edwards workforce. Both concepts have since gained traction at other bases and spread throughout the military.

Additionally, they have masterminded another TEDx event, helped create a pace-setting STEM display at the Aerospace Valley Airshow that shattered records, and initiated a series of rapid, collaborative activities, known as Hackathons, to solve a myriad of problems. Furthermore, they have stewarded the successful progression of projects initiated before their tenure, like Project FoX, T-7 remote testing, and Space Test Pilot School and transitioned them into sustainable initiatives. And, they have replicated themselves through multiple generations while providing a great example of leadership that unleashes a workforce and ignites innovation.

There was an additional benefit of our innovation journey and cultural transformation that has only been apparent in hindsight. Our innovation fervor and transformation pathway have replicated themselves in other locations, both through our example and via our alumni network that has carried our culture with them. This pathway of replication and sustainability is a prime example of a plan for continuing advantage!

The alumni stories are compelling and plentiful. The leaders of the Hustle Squad have moved on to make huge innovation-related impacts in other areas of the government and beyond. Heidi Williams left Edwards to bring her innovation passion to AFWERX and then Honeywell. Carlie Mensen, the second Hustle Squad lead, translated her experience at Edwards to a position serving at MITRE as a part of the famed Massachusetts Institute of Technology community. Cherie Head, the third Hustle Squad lead is still at Edwards providing a brilliant dose of continuity to her Hustle Squad successors. Britney Reed, the fourth Hustle Squad lead, has taken a position in Florida creating a new organization that merges Air Force data, autonomy, artificial intelligence and innovation to shape the future of warfare. The current Edwards innovation lead, Crosby Shaterian, proudly walks in their footsteps and still sees Edwards as the clear pacesetter for innovation in the Air Force. These innovation leaders are thriving while bringing unique backgrounds to new organizations as eyewitnesses to the power of an unleashed workforce and the potency of a *listen, consider* and *act* cycle.

Enlisted leaders are thriving as well. Chief RJ Jones moved from Edwards to a high-impact position in the Pentagon, revolutionizing the career pathway for all enlisted members of the Air Force. He has since retired and moved his family back to Edwards while taking a leadership position at the NASA Armstrong Flight Research Center. At NASA, he plays a major leadership role in helping guide the testing of two ground-breaking experimental aircraft—a reliable all-electric aircraft and a supersonic transport prototype that shapes the shock waves so that they minimize noise on the ground.

About a year after I left Edwards, Chief Ian Eishen moved on to an influential position working in the Air Force's Strategic Studies Group. There he directed policy for emerging technology and innovation and coordinated activity with key allies in Europe and the Pacific. He has also since retired and is working for a company in the Google portfolio orchestrating revolutionary networks and data-delivery systems through laser communications that are providing world-shaping connectivity. These leaders have used their Edwards experience to tackle the world. Their stories are just a fraction of the power of a thriving alumni network.

CHAPTER SEVENTEEN ♣ **CONTINUING ADVANTAGE** | 173

As mentioned in the prologue, Sergeant Michael Meyer has brought a cutting-edge mindset about virtual and augmented reality (VR/AR) to the training enterprise for the entire United States Air Force, molding the future of warfare support activities. The innovation experience at Edwards metamorphosized him from a disgruntled member of the workforce who was on the verge of quitting into a visionary leader and a VR/AR prophet. He is also planning a base wide TEDx event to impact his new location, like he did for our team at Edwards, and is a regular invitee to innovation activities and wargaming exercises around the Department of Defense. Meyer "grew up in a world where younger people weren't valued and couldn't make a real impact." But according to Meyer, the innovation experience at Edwards "gave [him]the tools to chase the future. It created a higher calling in [his] life, a call to duty."

Sergeant Jeremy Neilson is a new dad and thriving member of the Space Force. As he reflects on his unorthodox proposal in the VR/AR lab, he sees it as a symbolic expression of his transition into becoming a new person. He marvels that the innovation journey allowed someone who had grown up in a small Colorado town to become a "whole person" at work and in his personal life. "I was able to solidify who I was," says Neilson, "in pursuit of a life of fulfillment." And as he launches off into follow-on military service in the Space Force, he sees a direct link between the spirit of our innovation journey at Edwards and the rich legacy of our nation's founders.

Sergeant Chad Hardesty is now proudly wearing his TEST patch daily to the Pentagon in the Talent Management Innovation Cell and as a part of an Air Force strategic innovation and incubation element called Morpheus, attempting to "unleash the power within" the entire service's workforce. Up until his time at Edwards, he felt like "no one would listen" to him or to others. He was a faceless, nameless cog in the wheel of a big bureaucracy. But after witnessing the innovation journey at Edwards and seeing it "spark life into the entire population," he "felt like anything was possible." He recognized that he had individual value because leaders were *listening*, and *considering*, and *acting*.

Tracy Kidder wrote *The Soul of a New Machine*, a classic book about technology development and innovation leadership. It provides a detailed account of the creation of a next-generation personal computer in the early 1980s that was named Eagle, created by a small cadre of experts at Data General calling themselves The Eclipse Group. It chronicles the demanding environment of such innovative pursuits and highlights the leadership characteristics of the Eclipse leader Tim West. After extensive research and interviews with the team, the author provides the reader with the following thought-provoking conclusions:

- *"For even the most potentially interesting jobs to be meaningful, there must be managers who are willing to throw away the management handbooks and take some risk."*

- *"More than two dozen people worked on [the Eagle] overtime, without any real hope of material rewards, for a year and a half; and afterward most of them felt glad. That happened largely because West and the other managers gave them enough freedom to invent, while at the same time guiding them towards success."*

One particular interview by the author was the most interesting and compelling. The interviewee was Rosemarie Seale, known as the "mother of the team." Officially she was the Eclipse secretary, but West allowed her to play a more extensive role than her positional title would indicate. About her boss, Seale says the following:

"He set up the opportunity and he didn't stand in anyone's way. He wasn't out there patting people on the back. But I've been in the world too long and known too many bosses who won't allow you the opportunity. He never put one restriction on me. Tom allowed me to take a role where I could make things happen. What does a secretary do? She types, answers the phone, and doesn't put herself out too much. He let me go out and see what I could get done. You see, he allowed me to be more than a secretary there."

Seale powerfully concluded her thoughts about the Eclipse experience, saying, "I would do it again. I would be very grateful to do it again. I think I would take a cut in pay to do it again."

Leaders in every corner of our society need to rip up the management handbooks that are hindering us and constraining our teams. Instead, we need dynamic leaders, not stagnant managers. Throughout our society, we are seeking leaders who are willing to be different. We need those motivated to have fun and take reasonable risk. We need those who are passionate about genuine care and concern and dedicated to helping their team members become the best possible versions of themselves. We need those who are eager to unleash their teams while activating the *listen, consider,* and *act* cycle. After all, that type of culture drove Tim West's team and many others to success.

West's team wanted the freedom to invent. They wanted a leader who would not stand in their way. They wanted opportunity. They wanted to be known for more than just their job title. They wanted an environment where the leader would *listen, consider,* and *act.* They wanted to be unleashed! And if they were, then they would do it all over again with a cut in their pay, a meaningful purpose in their heart, and a smile on their face.

Our alumni network from the innovation journey at Edwards would echo these thoughts. Sergeants Meyer, Neilson, and Hardesty would do so, and are boldly and creatively carrying innovative concepts forward into their new roles. Sergeant Hardesty reflects on his experience, saying, "I now see possibilities in all areas of my life. This is who I am. I spent my whole life in a box. I don't see boxes anymore, but open fields instead."

Heidi, Carlie, Cherie, and Britney would do so as well, as would RJ and Ian. Cherie reminisced about her time on the Hustle Squad, saying, "That one year was the time of my life. It turned me into a leader." Heidi states that "it was one of the pinnacle moments of not just my career, but my life." About the life-changing impact of the Edwards innovation journey, Carlie reflects that "I now approach everyone differently, in and out of work." Britney emphasizes that "innovation creates hope" and her experience at Edwards revealed to her that "all of a sudden, I had something to believe in." My long-term friend and Senior Innovation Council mainstay Tony Rubino definitively states that "our innovation journey changed my life forever." Boom!

Impacted in this revolutionary, life-changing way, these innovation alumni continue breaking barriers, challenging convention, and igniting innovation with their lives in full afterburner. Unlike these amazing, unleashed innovators from our organizational experiment at The Center of the Aerospace Testing Universe, Harry R. Truman remains buried at the base of Mount Saint Helens, a permanent symbol of the consequences of complacency.

In a world erupting with change, every leader should remember that mountains can, indeed, hurt you. Don't get buried by the evolving industry around you. Seize the initiative, lead well, break down the barriers of success, and innovate boldly to propel yourself, and your organization, to the edge of the envelope. Boom!

ENDNOTES

Prologue—A Hypothetical Wartime Scenario, Saved by Innovation

- Pg 2. *Agile Combat Employment (ACE):* For more details on the concept of ACE, please see: https://www.doctrine.af.mil/Portals/61/documents/AFDN_1-21/AFDN%201-21%20ACE.pdf

Introduction

- Pg 5. *"The mountain ain't going to hurt me"*: https://corvidsketcher.com/2022/07/14/harry-r-truman/

- Pg 8. *Figure 1.0:* The x-axis (horizontal) in Figure 1.0 displays the dates of innovation activity. The y-axis (vertical) represents the amount of innovation activity during that period of time (based on innovative ideas, creative comments, and voting activity).

- Pg 9. *Global $7.8 trillion problem:* https://www.gallup.com/workplace/393497/world-trillion-workplace-problem.aspx

Chapter 1—Breaking Glass

- Pg 11. *Muroc Gunnery Range:* https://www.aftc.af.mil/News/On-This-Day-in-Test-History/Article-Display-Test-History/Article/2210225/june-21-1940-muroc-gunnery-range-officially-activated/

- Pg 12. *Chuck Yeager did not start out his life that telegraphed fame and glory: Yeager,* Chuck Yeager and Leo Janos, 1985, p. 17.

- Pg 12. *"We didn't know if we could break the sound barrier"*: *101 Chuck Yeager-isms: Wit & Wisdom from America's Hero,* Chuck and Victoria Yeager, 2022, p. 86.

- Pg 12. *"commit itself to achieving the goal, before this decade is out"*: https://www.jfklibrary.org/asset-viewer/archives/JFKWHA/1961/JFKWHA-032/JFKWHA-032

- Pg 13. *"But why, some say, the Moon?"*: https://www.jfklibrary.org/learn/about-jfk/historic-speeches/address-at-rice-university-on-the-nations-space-effort

- Pg 14. *"Transformation is hard work and prevailing wisdom suggests that it takes years or maybe decades to adjust an underlying organizational culture."*: John Kotter, *What Leaders Really Do*, 1990, pg 88—it is a process that can take 5 to 10 years—and Kotter, *Leading Change*, 1996, pg 143—it plays out over years not months—maybe as long as a decade.

- Pg 16. *The USAF has a regulation covering the writing and interpretation of regulations:* DAFI 33-360 was replaced by DAFI 90-160 in April 2022.

Chapter 2—Street Signs and Quick Wins

- Pg 21. *"Never let them name a street after you at Edwards.":* 101 Chuck Yeager-isms: Wit & Wisdom from America's Hero, 2022, p. 126.
- Pg 21. *"The old-timers at Edwards":* Yeager, 1985, p. 237.
- Pg 22. "The most responsible job in military aviation": *Yeager,* 1985, p. 113.
- Pg 24. "WARNING: WITHOUT GENUINE CONCERN THIS IS ALL WORTHLESS": *The Passion of Command: The Moral Imperative of Leadership*, BP McCoy, 2007.
- Pg 25. *Steve Magness' book: Do Hard Things: Why We Get Resilience Wrong and the Surprising Science of Real Toughness,* Steve Magness, 2022, p. 242.
- Pg 25: *The track conclusion:* "Mental Toughness, Servant Leadership, and the Collegiate Distance Runner," 2012, Christopher S. Hammer, https://dc.ewu.edu/theses/32/
- Pg 25: *The conclusion was amplified by a study of over a thousand office workers:* "The Effect of Respect: Respectful Communication at Work Drives Resiliency, Engagement, and Job Satisfaction among Early Career Employees," 2021, Danielle LaGree, Brian Houston, Margaret Duffy, and Haejung Shin, https://journals.sagepub.com/doi/abs/10.1177/23294884211016529
- Pg 25: *The global pandemic of disengaged employees:* https://www.gallup.com/workplace/393497/world-trillion-workplace-problem.aspx

Chapter 3—Unleashing the Team

- Pg 29. *Dr. John Stapp stories:* https://www.nmspacemuseum.org/inductee/john-p-stapp/ and https://en.wikipedia.org/wiki/John_Stapp
- Pg 31. *X-15:* https://www.thisdayinaviation.com/tag/mach-6/#:~:text=9%20November%201961%3A%20Major%20Robert,and%20Bob%20White's%2011th%20flight.

Chapter 4—Sufficient Runway

- Pg 39. *Pancho Barnes and the nuclear-powered bomber: Edwards AFB: Then and Now,* 2001, p. 102 and https://en.wikipedia.org/wiki/Nuclear-powered_aircraft
- Pg 42. *116-Day Innovation Blitz:* https://www.edwards.af.mil/News/Commentaries/Display/Article/1635817/116-day-innovation-blitz/

Chapter 5—The Calendar and the Checkbook

- Pg 45. *The SR-71 Blackbird: Skunkworks,* Ben Rich, 1994, p. 327. There is some ambiguity about the naming of the Blackbird. Please see the following for a counter-narrative: https://theaviationgeekclub.com/sr-71-or-rs-71-how-the-legendary-blackbird-got-her-designation/

- Pg 46. *Self-persuasion: Think Again: The Power of Knowing What You Don't Know,* Adam Grant, 2021, p. 112 and "The Power of Self-Persuasion," Elliot Aronson, American Psychologist, 1999, p. 875-84.

- Pg 48. *"A commander meets to talk to his men to inspire them"*: *American Generalship: Character Is Everything: The Art of Command,* Edgar Puryear, 2000, p. 78.

- Pg 49. *Herb Kelleher and Southwest Airlines: Nuts: Southwest Airlines' Crazy Recipe for Business and Personal Success,* Kevin and Jackie Freiberg, 1996, p. 146.

- Pg 50. *Our Most Precious Resource:* "Our Most Precious Resource," Desert Wings, June 2011, https://www.edwards.af.mil/News/Commentaries/Display/Article/396682/leaders-forum-our-most-precious-resource/

Chapter 6—Charging the Hill

- Pg 53. *On December 17th, 1777*: https://founders.archives.gov/documents/Washington/03-12-02-0566

- Pg 56. *The F-35 program office:* https://www.af.mil/News/Article-Display/Article/1799701/aerial-refueling-probe-light-evaluations-flown-with-kc-135-effort-to-clear-navy/

- Pg 57. *Sprints: Sprint: How to Solve Big Problems and Test New Ideas in Just Five Days,* Jake Knapp, 2016, p 5-6.

Chapter 7—Dad Jokes

- Pg 61. *Eric "Winkle" Brown: Wings On My Sleeve,* Eric Brown, 2006, p. 95 and "Charles Lindberg Memorial Lecture Series," Smithsonian National Air and Space Museum, May 18, 2000.

- Pg 63. *The Military Commander and the Law:* https://www.afjag.af.mil/Portals/77/documents/Publications/MCL%202022_f.pdf?ver=U1fs1Sm6-eD2TiKqMyTWTw%3D%3D

- Pg 63. *Matt Emmons:* https://www.usatoday.com/story/sports/olympics/2016/07/08/emmons-no-stranger-to-adversity/86879070/https://en.wikipedia.org/wiki/Matthew_Emmons

- Pg 66. *AFWERX:* https://www.af.mil/News/Article-Display/Article/1254932/air-force-opens-doors-to-universities-small-businesses-and-entrepreneurs-to-boo/ and https://www.afwerx.af.mil/
- Pg 67. *Jason Korman and Gapingvoid:* I am currently the Executive Advisor of Innovation and Leadership for this unique company that helps leaders intentionally design their organizational culture to deliver sustained operational excellence while fostering a real, human, emotional, immersive connection to work, https://www.gapingvoid.com/

Chapter 8—An Innovation Manifesto

- Pg 71. *The Ernst Udet Story: The Aviators: Eddie Rickenbacker, Jimmy Doolittle, Charles Lindberg and the Epic Age of Flight,* Winston Groom, 2013, p. 183-85, 197-98, 280-87.
- Pg 72. *The Innovation Manifesto Video:* https://www.dvidshub.net/video/654778/412th-test-wing-manifesto-innovation
- Pg 74. *So soon as prudence has begun to grow up in the brain:* https://quotefancy.com/quote/992831/Robert-Louis-Stevenson-So-soon-as-prudence-has-begun-to-grow-up-in-the-brain-like-a
- Pg 77. *Relentless Socialization and the Culture Wall:* Thought from Gapingvoid, https://www.gapingvoid.com/
- Pg 78. *Memes/Memetics:* https://en.wikipedia.org/wiki/Memetics
- Pg 78. *Thomas Kuhn and Paradigms: The Structure of Scientific Revolutions, Thomas Kuhn,* 1962, p. 113, 11, 77.

Chapter 9—#innovativeAF (AF means Air Force)

- Pg 81. *The Office of Strategic Studies (OSS):* https://archive.org/details/SimpleSabotageFieldManual/page/n9/mode/2up
- Pg 89. *TEDx at Edwards:* https://www.aerotechnews.com/edwardsafb/2019/11/18/first-tedx-edwards-afb-sparks-innovation-discussion/
- Pg 92. "If you are looking for perfect safety": http://www.quoteswise.com/orville-wright-quotes-4.html
- Pg 93. *Holes below the waterline: How The Mighty Fall: And Why Some Companies Never Give In,* Jim Collins, 2009, p. 74.
- Pg 94. *Retweeting:* During the writing process of this book, Elon Musk changed the name of Twitter to X. Even under the new name, posts on X are still often called tweets or retweets. And, they certainly were called that under the original Twitter name.

Chapter 10—Spikes On A Wire

- Pg 97. *Smithsonian Magazine:* "Ten Inventions that Inadvertently Transformed Warfare," Mark Strauss, Sept 18, 2010, https://www.smithsonianmag.com/history/ten-inventions-that-inadvertently-transformed-warfare-62212258/
- Pg 99. *Psychological Moonshot:* Rory Sutherland, *Alchemy: The Dark Art and Curious Science of Creating Magic in Brands, Business, and Life,* p. 69.
- Pg 103. *Samuel Langley vs. the Wright Brothers:* https://blogs.scientificamerican.com/observations/why-did-the-wright-brothers-succeed-when-others-failed/#:~:text=The%20Wright%20Flyer%20cost%20the,profits%20from%20their%20bicycle%20business and The Wright Brothers, David McCullough, 2015, p. 108.

Chapter 11—A Message in the Misfortunes

- Pg 109. *Supreme Court John Roberts' Graduation Speech:* https://time.com/4845150/chief-justice-john-roberts-commencement-speech-transcript/
- Pg 110. *Thomas Edison's fire:* https://www.businessinsider.com/thomas-edison-in-the-obstacle-is-the-way-2014-5
- Pg 110. *Thomas Watson at IBM:* Many sources of varying quotes, reflecting a loss of $600,000 to $10 million.
- Pg 111. *Steve Magness' research on toughness: Do Hard Things: Why We Get Resilience Wrong and the Surprising Science of Real Toughness,* Steve Magness, 2022, p. 13.
- Pg 111. *Carol Dweck's growth and fixed mindset: Mindset: The New Psychology of Success,* Carol Dweck, 2006.
- Pg 116. *The Grit Award:* https://www.edwards.af.mil/News/Article/1891582/air-traffic-controller-receives-grit-award/

Chapter 12—Trial By Dragon

- Pg 119. *Frederick Douglass: The Speeches of Frederick Douglass,* Ed. By John McKivigan, Julie Husband, Heather Kaufman, 2018, p. 533-4.
- Pg 123. *Culture Walls:* Thought from Gapingvoid, https://www.gapingvoid.com/
- Pg 124. *President Theodore Roosevelt Quote: Leadership in Turbulent Times,* Doris Kearns Goodwin, 2018, p. 265.
- Pg 124. *Talk with Team Teichert:* https://www.facebook.com/watch/live/?ref=watch_permalink&v=230206064577440
- Pg 126. *Project FoX:* https://www.af.mil/News/Article-Display/Article/2577421/reserve-airman-makes-history-with-innovative-project-foxf-

35-development/ and https://www.airandspaceforces.com/f-22-flies-with-third-party-apps-new-open-software-architecture/

Chapter 13—Non-Material Solutions

- Pg 129. *Yeager Story about TPS: Yeager*, 1985, p. 237, p. 216–219.
- Pg 133. *Winter of Waivers/Boston Tea Party:* https://www.edwards.af.mil/News/Commentaries/Display/Article/2042536/a-magnificent-movement/
- Pg 135. *"Rules are made for those unwilling to make up their own": 101 Chuck Yeager-isms: Wit & Wisdom from America's Hero*, 2022, p. 9.

Chapter 14—Shared Humanity and Mutual Benefit

- Pg 137. *Spain and France commitment to the American revolutionary cause:* https://www.sar.org/wp-content/uploads/2020/06/Spain-in-the-American-Revolution-by-Stephen-Renouf.pdf
- Pg 141. *F-16 crash:* https://www.wusa9.com/article/news/local/maryland/hero-pilot-told-wife-i-love-you-before-safely-ejecting-from-fighter-jet/65-496843862
- Pg 144. *These lessons were still fresh in my mind:* Teichert's farewell to JBA: https://bizroundtable.org/farewell-from-colonel-e-john-teichert-commander-11th-wing-joint-base-andrews/
- Pg 146. *The Collier Trophy:* https://www.flyingmag.com/f35-technology-wins-collier-trophy/
- Pg 148. *I was beaming with pride when President Biden:* https://www.militarytimes.com/news/your-military/2023/01/06/its-official-military-spouses-to-get-employment-relief-after-moving/

Chapter 15—Your Greatest Idea

- Pg 151. *On June 3rd, 1980, unbeknownst to the vast majority of humanity: Raven Rock*, 2017, Garrett M. Graff, p. 263.
- Pg 154. *Unskilled and Unaware:* "Unskilled and Unaware of It: How Difficulties in Recognizing One's Own Incompetence Lead to Inflated Self-Assessments," David Dunning and Justin Kruger, *Journal of Personality and Social Psychology*, Jan 2000.

Chapter 16—Daring Wins!

- Pg 159. *Test pilot, inventor, and innovator Wilbur Wright: The Wright Brothers,* David McCullough, 2015, p 48.
- Pg 159. *French visionary Louis Pierre Mouillard: The Empire of the Air,* Louis-Pierre Mouillard, 1881, p. 463.

- Pg 160. In Chapter 8, I briefly described the concept and power of paradigms: *The Structure of Scientific Revolutions,* Thomas Kuhn, 1962, p. 144.
- Pg 167. "An arrogant pilot will get ya killed; confident ones make history": *101 Chuck Yeager-isms: Wit & Wisdom from America's Hero,* 2022, p. 4.
- Pg 167. *"Those only are happy who have their minds fixed on some object other than their own happiness"*: *Think Again: The Power of Knowing What You Don't Know,* Adam Grant, 2021, p. 112.

Chapter 17—Continuing Advantage
- Pg 170. I once had an eccentric strategy professor Dr Everett Dolman: *Pure Strategy: Power and Principle in the Space and Information Age,* Everett Dolman, 2005, p. 6, 12.
- Pg 173. Tracy Kidder quotes: *The Soul of a New Machine,* Tracy Kidder, 1981, p. 274-275.

ACKNOWLEDGMENTS

Writing this book was unexpectedly enjoyable. It provided me with a refreshing and encouraging memory of the amazing people I have served alongside of during my life and career.

I want to begin by thanking my Lord and Savior, Jesus Christ, for all the blessings in my life. I also want to thank my amazing family, Team Teichert, that includes my remarkable wife, Melonie, and our incredible children, Summer, Tiffany, and Noah. I love you and continue to deeply enjoy serving alongside of you!

I want to thank all the Airmen, Soldiers, Sailors, Marines, Guardians, and Coast Guardsmen who have supported and defended the Constitution of the United States—past, present, and future. This book contains a small portion of the richness of my interaction with you. I especially want to thank the team at The Center of the Aerospace Testing Universe and the community in the Aerospace Valley. I mentioned a few names in this book, but there are so many more who played a significant role in our massive innovation movement. I hope that you recognize your part in this compelling story as it unfolds on the pages of this book!

I deeply appreciate those who substantially shaped this book throughout the writing process. Thank you to John Stenbeck who reached out on LinkedIn and offered a valuable, unsolicited perspective on the authorship and publishing process. Thank you, as well, to Michael Abrashoff whose book, It's Your Ship, inspired me to tell my own story of organizational transformation. A huge additional thanks to Jack Hellmann for his invaluable mentorship during my transition from the military and for encouraging me to write a book that would make my family proud.

I also deeply appreciate Lauren Mix, the best and most timely editor in the business, for her masterful help in molding this book into a quality final product. I am also grateful for Jeremy and Alyssa Lofgren for creating a masterful cover design and a wonderful overall format.

I am humbled, honored, privileged, and blessed to have served our great nation in the United States Air Force. I truly hope this book adequately reflects a journey that can inspire others to greater effectiveness in their own leadership context. Today, our world desperately needs the right kind of leaders. Lead well!

ABOUT THE AUTHOR

Brigadier General John "Dragon" Teichert, United States Air Force (retired)

John is a recently-retired brigadier general, a national security expert, and a leadership champion. He has vast whole-of-government leadership experience that includes military, diplomatic, intelligence, and industrial instruments of power—from cutting-edge technology to our nation's most sensitive international relationships. Throughout John's career, his unique, fun-loving leadership style, infused with a heartfelt love of country, true passion for people, and burning desire for progress, has relentlessly unshackled the creativity and talent of teams at all levels.

Growing up in the Pacific northwest, John had an early passion for service to his country, with the movie TOP GUN cementing his desire to fly fast jets and live a life on the edge of the danger zone. He earned engineering degrees from the Massachusetts Institute of Technology and Stanford University before swearing his oath to support and defend the Constitution of the United States via the United States Air Force.

While John relished his Air Force flying assignments, he quickly grew far more interested in becoming an inspirational, innovative, and integrity-filled leader. His leadership approach has been developed by leaders who intentionally invested in him but also by those whose style was the antithesis of the model to which John aspired.

John ended his service to the Air Force as the Assistant Deputy Undersecretary of the Air Force, International Affairs, responsible for world-wide international engagement on behalf of the U.S. Air Force and U.S. Space Force while leading the services' entire $240 billion security cooperation portfolio. Prior to that, John was the Senior Defense Official and Defense Attaché to Iraq, leading on the front lines of whole-of-government national security strategy and policy in the most challenging of conditions.

John has been an F-15E combat pilot and F-22 test pilot, and commanded Joint Base Andrews and Edwards Air Force Base. He has written extensively and spoken globally on leadership, innovation, risk management, national security, security cooperation, and international affairs. Additionally, he is the founder and president of Capital Leadership LLC, passionately developing the leaders our nation needs.

Currently, he is a U.S. Senate candidate out of the great state of Maryland. His eclectic activities can best be followed through johnteichert.com, teichertformaryland.com and LinkedIn as he continues to serve with his amazing wife Melonie and their three remarkable children.